T0360457

# Youth Unemployment Scenarios

This book examines the factors driving youth unemployment in South Africa, exploring potential future outcomes of its mass unemployment, and offering a variety of strategies to avoid an impending crisis in the country.

Utilizing scenario analysis rooted in complex systems theory while building on statistical and field research, the author illustrates four possible future states of youth employment in South Africa in the year 2040. This includes the South African version of the Arab Spring, where young people riot or agitate for extreme political and social change because of a belief that access to education and jobs is only possible through social status or corruption (Spring), fair access to a high number of jobs supported by Chinese interventions (Summer), a technology-driven decline in the number of jobs where merit-based access for youth is granted (Fall), and the collapse of the economy, with the economy collapsing and youth becoming increasingly desperate (Winter). The author then presents five strategies to fight youth unemployment, including training of youth to start businesses, stimulating small- and medium-sized enterprises, and sending unemployed youth abroad for skills development and to where their labour is needed.

This book will be of interest to scholars of South African politics and economics, labour economics and youth studies, and readers with an interest in tackling youth unemployment independent of the country.

**Maximilian Matschke** was born and raised in Munich, Germany. He attained a Bachelor's degree and a Master's degree in Technology and Management from the Technical University in Munich, and subsequently completed an Honours degree in Technology Management, spending a term abroad at Columbia Business School in New York, and doing internships in Germany, Singapore, China, and Spain. Max started three social ventures, all addressing the issue of youth employment. The first of these, founded in 2011, was a student-run consulting firm in Johannesburg, The Consulting Academy Johannesburg, which later expanded to Cape Town, Nairobi, and Guadalajara. The second was an entrepreneurship boot camp for unemployed youth, which was successfully piloted and used as a base for a train-the-trainer approach. The third, uNowanga, is an upskilling initiative done in collaboration with the international charity, St John, South Africa. It is a programme to send unemployed youth from South Africa to Germany to train as nurses. He interrupted his career in consulting to pursue a doctorate on youth employment in South Africa. The resulting PhD formed the basis for this book.

# Youth Unemployment Scenarios
## South Africa in 2040

**Maximilian Matschke**

Routledge
Taylor & Francis Group

LONDON AND NEW YORK

First published 2023
by Routledge
4 Park Square, Milton Park, Abingdon, Oxon OX14 4RN

and by Routledge
605 Third Avenue, New York, NY 10158

*Routledge is an imprint of the Taylor & Francis Group, an informa business*

*British Library Cataloguing-in-Publication Data*
A catalogue record for this book is available from the British Library

*Library of Congress Cataloging-in-Publication Data*
Names: Matschke, Maximilian, 1989– author.
Title: Youth unemployment scenarios : South Africa in 2040 /
Maximilian Matschke.
Other titles: Routledge contemporary South Africa.
Description: New York : Routledge, 2023. |
Series: Routledge contemporary South Africa |
Includes bibliographical references and index. |
Identifiers: LCCN 2022018448 | ISBN 9781032029627 (hardback) |
ISBN 9781032029665 (paperback) | ISBN 9781003186052 (ebook)
Subjects: LCSH: Unemployed youth–South Africa–Forecasting. |
Youth–Employment–South Africa Forecasting. |
Youth–Employment–Government policy–South Africa. |
Youth–South Africa–Economic conditions. | Employment forecasting–
South Africa. | South Africa–Economic conditions–1991–
Classification: LCC HD6276.S6 M38 2023 | DDC 331.341370968–dc23
LC record available at https://lccn.loc.gov/2022018448

ISBN: 978-1-032-02962-7 (hbk)
ISBN: 978-1-032-02966-5 (pbk)
ISBN: 978-1-003-18605-2 (ebk)

DOI: 10.4324/9781003186052

Typeset in Times New Roman
by Newgen Publishing UK

# Contents

# Figures

# Preface

I first encountered South Africa during my bachelor degree when I took a term off to travel abroad. One of my projects was to start the first student-run consulting firm in South Africa. I worked with several South African students and many others from Sub-Saharan Africa. The one thing about them that stayed with me was their eagerness to succeed, an observation that would lead me to a world of research and enquiry in South Africa that started with a PhD on South Africa's largest mid-term challenge: youth unemployment. This research later became the basis for this book. I learned about the significant challenges faced by young people, and I was taken aback by the vast contrasts of experiences and perspectives facing young South Africans compared to my own experiences and those of my peers growing up in Germany and the United States.

Having grown up outside South Africa and in very different cultural environments, there is no doubt that my world view differs significantly from that of someone raised in an informal settlement in South Africa. This made field research imperative in order to understand the context of the people I was studying, and to add to the numerical context and expert opinions that also formed part of the research. My aim was to gain a holistic perspective on the experiences of young people in South Africa, with a specific focus on youth employment and unemployment.

The locus of the research was the township communities in South Africa, given that this is the heartland of unemployment in the country.

It was imperative for me, as a white foreigner, to do my fieldwork with respect, humility, and a self-awareness that would enable me to be cognisant of cultural, racial, and ethical sensitivities in engaging with South Africans. I travelled to the townships with a black South African guide, addressing youth groups unknown to me with the intention of understanding their lives, challenges, and hopes.

My aim was not to impose myself or my pre-conceptions or opinions on the subjects of study. It was rather to focus on the story of South Africa's youth and the challenges they face. The main objective was to share the narrative of the youth with the public who would read my research study and, later, the book.

Ensuring a youth-centred narrative required me to seek opinions, ask frank questions, and create room for questions to enable me to probe and clarify the issues in depth. The fieldwork was an exceptionally positive experience. Every single participant was keen to engage and to share his or her story.

The research was supervised by Professor Dr Helmut Asche, Honorary Professor at the Johannes Gutenberg-Universität Mainz, Germany; Dr Hylton White, Senior Lecturer at the University of the Witwatersrand in Johannesburg, South Africa; and Professor Johann Maree, Emeritus Professor at the University of Cape Town, South Africa.

# Acknowledgements

A special thanks goes to:

- My supervisors Helmut, Hylton, and Johann, for guiding me and critically challenging my ambitious work.
- Louis van der Merwe, who opened my eyes to the magic of scenario planning in 2011, motivating me to pursue a PhD, years before I started my work.
- Roche Diagnostics (Pty) Ltd for the financial support for this project.
- My previous employer, for granting me a sabbatical to follow my passion and for financially supporting me.
- All those who helped me gain access to the people I engaged with, namely Lucky and the Centre for Development and Enterprise.
- Ashor, who has kept me motivated to write in many productive and enjoyable writing sessions.
- Lastly, and most importantly, my parents who enabled me to get where I am now and who supported me along the way.

# Introduction

Youth unemployment in South Africa is a ticking time bomb. About half of the working-age population under the age of 34 does not have a job. Without a job, there is no income. Without an income, there is no way to build a future. The Arab Spring, a civil uprising that started in Tunisia and spread across parts of the Arab world in the early 2010s taking down a number of corrupt and autocratic regimes along the way, vividly illustrated the potential consequences of widespread dissatisfaction among socioeconomically desperate young people.

The uprising was a reminder that the future is anything but predictable. What does the future of South Africa look like considering its masses of desperate, unemployed, and unskilled youth? Is there a way to disarm this ticking time bomb, and how could we prepare for the possibility of its detonation?

This is a topic that is frequently discussed in South Africa but answers to these and many other questions related to the problem are hard to find.

Why is this the case? It is partly because many of those who discuss the issues in the public sphere know there is a problem, but they are too far away from the genesis of it to understand its complexity and to understand what those directly affected believe should happen.

The voices being heard are mostly not those of the affected youth from disadvantaged backgrounds. Those who are most affected lack a voice and a platform to articulate the problems and contribute to finding solutions. Policy makers tend to avoid forums or conferences where these issues are discussed and do not appear to be interested in contributing to them.

The focus of debates on the unemployment and related issues is on the cause of them. Reasons given by analysts, economists, and academics include the broken public education system, the destruction of university property by students, the economy, or government incompetence

DOI: 10.4324/9781003186052-1

and lack of policy vision. All of these are contributing factors, but none is a singular cause.

The discussions also tend to be isolated, addressing single issues contributing to youth unemployment in South Africa such as education or health or employers or social injustice. They tend to not be viewed holistically, as an interdependent combination of multiple causes.

For example, in a study conducted by a local independent public policy research and advocacy organisation, the Centre for Development and Enterprise (CDE), which included visits to 20 municipalities with the highest absolute youth unemployment, the more stimulating insights from the field research were omitted from the published report on its findings. Broadly, the solution offered focused on policies to stimulate economic growth.

Another example where young people were involved in the discussion was the highly regarded National Foundations Dialogue Initiative, supported by the foundations of Umlambo, Thabo Mbeki, Kgalema Motlanthe, Jakes Gerwel, Helen Suzman, FW de Klerk, Desmond and Leah Tutu Legacy, Chief Albert Luthuli, and the Robert Mangaliso Sobukwe Trust. It did come up with insights on how to give the youth a voice but did not deliver specific interventions that may have made a difference to the problem.

This book, through its detailed research and field work, aims to create an understanding of what youth unemployment actually looks like in the daily lives of young South Africans, dissecting the root causes of youth unemployment, understanding the drivers of employment, creating scenarios to illustrate what South Africa could look like by 2040, and most importantly, it examines what can be done in today's sociopolitical environment to create employment.

## Youth in the driving seat

The youth could be considered to be the driving force of the societies they stand to inherit. Young people tend to step up and create change when they are discontented with their circumstances. The North African region was generally regarded as being more stable and affluent than most of Sub-Saharan Africa until the so-called Arab Spring erupted, with the youth leading a revolution in which several entrenched governments in the region were pushed out through persistent street protests and other actions.

It was expected that similar uprisings would overflow into other regions in Africa, but this did not happen at the time. However, in Sudan, long-time ruler Omar Al-Bashir was also ousted in a similar fashion in 2019, toppled by long-running street protests led mostly by students.

In other countries led by autocratic leaders, such as Zimbabwe, protests have simply led to state crackdowns that have quelled the opposition. This raises a crucial question as to if and how the youth in sub-Saharan Africa might create substantive change. Will the youth be vanguards of change or vandals as academics Abbink and van Kassel proclaim, or the makers or breakers as described by the Africa anthropologists Honwana and Boeck?

Further questions proliferate in this regard. For example, what if all unemployed youth started working tomorrow, a hypothetical question posed by the International Labour Organization, a United Nations agency for labour-related matters. Would the gap between the poor and the rich narrow? Would African countries become more equal? What would be the impact on migration to countries outside Africa?

What would an increasingly disillusioned and unhappy youth population be prepared to do to change their circumstances? Would they see the forceful redistribution of wealth as a solution? Would that be a sustainable economic path? Would it divide, rather than unite, the continent?

Unemployment is Africa's biggest challenge according to Helen Zille, the former head of South Africa's main opposition party, the Democratic Alliance. This statement is worth a closer look.

Sustainable growth on the African continent is dependent on economic inclusion. Growth from exporting natural resources is not sustainable, as the high poverty levels across the continent show. Africa's working-age population is the fastest growing globally. By 2040, the continent will be home to the world's largest working population at about 1.1 billion, according to the McKinsey Global Institute, the consulting firm's think tank. But by 2021, the unemployment rate was already sky high, reaching a high of 59 percent in South Africa for example.

Enrolment numbers in African education lag other emerging markets, with the gap widening in recent years. Just over a third of the Sub-Saharan African population finish high school, and under 10 percent attend university. The willingness of the youth to migrate for economic reasons is high – up to 75 percent in Sierra Leone, for example. This means they will get educated but it does not solve the bigger problem.

The quality of employment for young people, where it exists, is often low and badly paid, with people in low paying jobs barely able to move out of poverty. Women earn less and are more likely to be unemployed. Socially excluded youth who have lost, or are at risk of losing, parental care face even bigger employment challenges.

The relevance of employment for the well-being of the world is visible in the United Nations Sustainable Development Goals, which were adopted as part of the 2030 Agenda for Sustainable Development in 2015 to emphasise a holistic approach to achieving sustainable development for all.

Five of the 17 goals are linked to employment, as follows: No poverty (Goal 1), quality education (Goal 4), gender equality (Goal 5), decent work and economic growth (Goal 8), and reduced inequality (Goal 10). Furthermore, the African Union Agenda 2063 highlights employment matters in Aspiration 6: "An Africa whose development is people-driven, relying on the potential of African people, especially its women and youth, and caring for children."

## Framing future employment for South African youth

The big issues in South Africa today include youth underemployment and unemployment, gender inequality, skills shortages, a lack of aspirations, and a lack of opportunity for people in marginalised communities. Economic growth is not keeping up with population growth and as a result, there are simply not enough jobs for school leavers and the many who are unemployed in the country. Economic development is dependent on tangible and intangible resources, and growth is not inclusive, nor is investment necessarily directed to areas of job creation at scale. The jobs that exist are often informal, attract low wages or are not accessible to people, depending on their background and social networks.

The combination of a growing youth population and a slow-growth economy is a recipe for trouble. South Africa is one of the most unequal societies in the world, with a growing gap between the rich and the poor. The implications of this on the livelihoods of today's youth and their children tomorrow are hard to predict. But the fact that this growing inequality and hardship might drive change is not unlikely.

The question is whether it will be a moderated change, driven by sound policies, or whether it will be revolutionary change, driven by poverty and marginalisation. The key to bridging this gap constructively way is certainly the youth. An income will give them a purpose, and hope for the future.

Using the metaphor of a time bomb for South Africa raises many questions. Why is there a bomb with a ticking detonator in the first place? How did it come to be there? What would happen if it exploded? How long is the timer set for before it detonates? Can it be defused? How? By whom?

These questions underpin this research, along with identifying drivers of employment, building scenarios for youth employment by 2040, highlighting existing initiatives and ideas for tackling the problem, and proposing original solutions. Only a holistic view of youth unemployment using data; expert analysis; and field work that cuts across economics, systems thinking, and sociological and anthropological fields, will shed the necessary light on these issues from different angles in the search for solutions.

The questions this research clarifies therefore are:

- What is the status quo of youth unemployment in South Africa, considering both perceptions of the situation as well as statistics?
- What are the drivers inhibiting employment creation?
- What is the path to youth employment in South Africa?
- What could youth employment look like in South Africa in 2040?
- Which measures will help to support youth employment?

These are broad topics, but the research did aim to draw a holistic picture of the current situation in South Africa and consider factors that may affect how it develops in future. It was necessary to set certain parameters in order to tackle the sheer size and diversity of this topic, and to illustrate its dynamics over a long timeframe. These were needed to provide a strong structure for the research and the capability to embed quantitative information, such as statistical data, as well as qualitative data, including implicit knowledge, observations, and opinions.

Furthermore, the framework needed to allow scenario planning. The results had to be easy to illustrate and comprehensible. The framework used often for developmental issues, policy making, raising awareness, and eventually triggering actions is scenario analysis, forms the foundation of this work.

## Key findings

The main challenges identified from the research are, broadly speaking:

- Fifty-nine percent of the youth in South Africa did not have a job at the time of the research, with the biggest cohort being among entrants to the job market.
- Job prospects are best in urban areas and in Western Cape Province, and worst in rural areas and Eastern Cape Province.
- Black Africans are disproportionately affected by unemployment compared to other ethnic groups in South Africa.

- There is a direct correlation between increased educational attainment and lower levels of unemployment and desperation.
- University graduates have a 95 percent chance of finding a job.
- Three-quarters of unemployed youth in South Africa have never worked before.
- One-third of employed youth have an informal job.
- Most workers earn a wage or salary.
- There is little extant entrepreneurial activity among the youth, with just 9 percent engaged in entrepreneurial activities.
- The youth hustle for low-paid work and are typically lacking the third-party support of personal networks or professional institutions.
- The challenges of finding a job vary but are primarily about a lack of access at to employment opportunities at a technological, social, and physical level.

Other findings included the fact that there is a lack of role models in the social environment of people interviewed, particularly in township areas; levels of contentment are low; and the willingness to engage in violent protest is high.

The book derives 11 drivers for employment in South Africa, each of which also has underlying drivers. These are:

1  Number of available jobs (most impactful driver): Growth in labour-intensive industries, substitution of jobs by technology, economic growth, and location of jobs.
2  Entrepreneurship: Confidence and mindset and access to entrepreneurship centres.
3  Demography: Demographic dividend, birth rate and fertility, mortality and expected age, and retirement age.
4  Migration: Migration in and beyond Africa, emigration or the brain drain, illegal immigration, and legal immigration.
5  Schooling: Learning practical skills in school, quality of education, access, and time in school.
6  Skills: Focus of training efforts, magnitude and transparency of efforts, and placement challenges.
7  Health: Childhood malnutrition, general healthcare, and poverty-related illness and diseases.
8  Access: Access to social ties, IT access and knowledge, as well as geographic access to jobs.
9  Employability barriers: Issues of qualifications and experience, the power of trade unions, and minimum wages and subsidies.

10  Social and cultural environment: Gender bias, substance abuse, and socialisation.
11  Perceived inclusion of youth (most uncertain driver): Perceived inclusion in job opportunities and perceived inclusion in education and in society.

There are four scenarios outlined in the book, characterised as Spring, Summer, Fall, and Winter, which span extremes that could possibly play out for the youth in South Africa. This includes the South African version of the Arab Spring, where young people riot or agitate for extreme political and social change because of a belief that access to education and jobs is only possible through social status or corruption (Spring), fair access to a high number of jobs (Summer), a decline in the number of jobs where merit-based access for youth is granted (Fall), and the collapse of the economy, with youth becoming increasingly desperate (Winter).

The book concludes by identifying five proposals for addressing youth unemployment that may help to avoid a Winter scenario unfolding in South Africa:

1  Boosting the economy in targeted geographies and industries.
2  Training youth to start a business.
3  Stimulating small- and medium-sized enterprises.
4  Sending unemployed and unskilled youth abroad for skills development and to where their labour is needed.
5  Implementing an employer-demand-led training model.

## Bibliography

Abbink, J., & van Kessel, I. (2005). Vanguard or vandals: Youth, politics, and conflict in Africa. African Dynamics: Vol. 4. Leiden; Boston, MA: Brill.

African Union (2015). *Agenda 2063: The Africa we want.*

Altbaker, A., & Bernstein, A. (2017). *No country for young people: The crisis of youth unemployment and what to do about it.* Johannesburg: CDE.

Asche, H. (2018). Neue deutsche Außenpolitik? In K. Andrejewski (Ed.), *Audit committee quarterly: Das Magazin für corporate governance* (2018th ed., pp. 36–37). Frankfurt a. M.: Audit Committee Institute.

Bernstein, A. (2017a). *Teacher professional standards for South Africa: The road to better performance, development and accountability?* Johannesburg: CDE.

Bernstein, A. (2017b, April). *Youth employment in South Africa.* Johannesburg: Centre for Development and Enterprise.

Canca, N. (2017, August 30). Interview by M. Matschke. Cape Town.

Cronje, F. (2014). *A time traveller's guide to our next ten years.* Cape Town: NB Publishers.

Honwana, A. M., & Boeck, F. d. (2005). *Makers & breakers, made & broken: Children & youth as emerging categories in postcolonial Africa*. Oxford: James Curry.

International Labour Organization (2016). *World employment and social outlook 2016: Trends for youth*. ILO Publications (online).

Koseff, S. (2018, August). *Education and youth employment: A priority for all South Africans*. Johannesburg: Gordon Institute of Business Science (GIBS).

McKinsey Global Institute (September 2016). *Lions on the move II: Realizing the potential of Africa's economies*. McKinsey & Company.

Nxasana, S. (2018, August). *Education and youth employment: A priority for all South Africans*. Johannesburg: Gordon Institute of Business Science (GIBS).

Pityana, B., & Canca, N. (2017, September 18). Interview by M. Matschke. Johannesburg.

Schirmer, S., & Bernstein, A. (2017). *Business, growth and inclusion: Tackling youth unemployment in cities, towns and townships*. Johannesburg: CDE.

Statistics South Africa (2021). *Quarterly labour force survey (2nd quarter 2021)*.

United Nations (2015). *Sustainable development goals: 17 goals to transform our world*.

Zille, H. (2016). *Not without a fight: The autobiography*. Cape Town: Penguin Random House South Africa.

# 1 Life of the unemployed youth across South Africa

It is often said that the best way to find out what people think is to ask them. South Africa's unemployment problem is not an esoteric or academic issue; it is a very real daily struggle for millions of people. It's not often that they are asked about their own experiences and fight for survival, even as their plight becomes part of regular statistics updates. So, the author visited several townships across South Africa to ask young residents about their lives and challenges in order to set the context for the research project that underpins this book. Here is their story.

## A slow day in Katlehong

Lesotho Street, in one of the informal settlements that make up the township of Katlehong outside Johannesburg, is long and straight. It is an immaculate relic of apartheid's spatial planning, which created segregated towns for black people, or in apartheid parlance, "non-whites," ensuring the separation of domiciles of "non-whites" from formal economic centres and from areas in which white people lived.

Lesotho Street intersects with Matsose Street in the middle of Katlehong, which lies 35 kilometres south-east of central Johannesburg and forms part of the city of Ekurhuleni. The western side of the road is crammed with tin shacks, while the seam of the eastern side is bordered by haphazardly placed public plastic toilets. The perfectly straight road is in sharp contrast to the chaos along its edges.

There is a one-story building, which has a street-facing wall constructed from five different and unaligned corrugated sheets. The roof is another sheet of tin. I sit in front of the building on the pavement, surrounded by sticky red dust. I look onto the side of the road with the grey and red toilets. In front of them is a puddle. Sewage and excrement emit a biting odour, carried in waves by the light breeze.

DOI: 10.4324/9781003186052-2

The government has clearly failed to provide sanitary facilities that can be used with dignity by those living in the area.

It is hot in the sun. The breeze makes the temperature tolerable but not the smell. I am the "black" sheep or the only white person – the odd one out – in a place where everyone else is black, and mostly Zulu. It does not look many white people visit or live here. People watch me as I sit on the pavement with my friend and guide, Lucky, who is a city councillor responsible for Katlehong.

The structural chaos does not seem to touch people here. Everything moves slowly. From time to time, a car drives past, slowly. An elderly woman washes clothes in a tin basin, slowly. A young man pulls a cart overfilled with empty plastic bottles, slowly.

Six young men sit in front of the shack next to me with its yellow porch and watch the road, their faces expressionless. They talk, slowly. I do not observe any strong emotions, no laughter, crying, nor anger. They seem to be in a state of waiting. Waiting for better times? Meanwhile, time goes by, slowly.

I look at the young men. They seem to be in their early twenties, and all very lean, except for one. My shorts have attracted a haze of red from the dust in the street, as have my shoes and t-shirt. But the young men are clean. Some of their clothing looks worn, but the white is white, the blue is blue, the yellow is yellow. Even the white soles of one man's Converse-style shoes are white.

The group of men sit so they can watch the street. Everything that happens here happens on the street. Nothing goes unnoticed by the five youths. They know everyone. It's their 'hood. They wave at people walking past and at cars.

Suddenly, a young man joins the group. He shakes everyone's hand, the African way: he stretches out his arms, palm reaches for palm, fingers pointing slightly downwards – so far, the international handshake. But then, palms stay connected, both hands move so that the fingers point slightly upwards, and then back. Fingers pointing down and a soft snap with each other's thumbs. Six times.

The energy in the group picks up and one man leaves to go into a nearby shack to fetch something. The group changes formation. They now face each other, turning their backs on the straight road. One makes a sweeping arm movement, as if he threw something. Then, the next one does the same distinct movement. Laughter. Then the next one. Now I see the dice, two of them. The men play for a while.

Then one young man nods his head towards me. Others follow, looking at me. Do I need to prepare to run? The man who points at me indicates that I should come over. I hesitate, then make my way

*Figure 1.1* Impressions from the field – the African handshake.
Source: Photo by Lucky Dinake.

towards them. The man who flagged me down extends his hand. We do
the African handshake. Then again, four times over. I sit down in their
circle. They want me to join the game. I try to understand the rules.
Their English is difficult to understand, but their rules are impossible:

> it's like three five or three one, the number that you say. I'm doing
> seven. Okay maybe [you] can say "okay, do six five me, it's 11",
> okay, they can say "four-four, and then when you do that four-four,
> and then you lose, they take the money… it's like that.

They ask me to put in money. One South African rand. I hesitate.
The smallest denomination I have is a R10 note. No coins. I politely
decline and ask to not play until I get the rules. No problem. I still do
not understand them. I try to link their cheering and moaning to the
numbers on the dice. No luck. They see that I am struggling.

*Figure 1.2* Impressions from the field – a street in Katlehong.
Source: Photos by Lucky Dinake.

I ask how often they play.

> It goes to mostly weekends. Maybe when the month is ending on Tuesday or Wednesday, then we start [earlier], maybe the month like this – like last month. It ends on Wednesday and then we start on Wednesday [and gamble] up until Sunday.

I am curious if they run it as a business or play for fun. One clarifies, "It's just to get a little money, you see? It's not a business." It costs R20 to get into the game. They tell me the story of the "one guy [that] ended up having two thousand."

I learn their names and ages: Themba, 22; Siyanda, 26; Lawrence, 32; Shepard, 29; and Vuyani, 24.

They ask after my business in town. I tell them I am studying youth unemployment in South Africa. They start telling me their stories. No one has a job. No one has matric. Some finished school in grade eight. Some tried to do their matric – the final-year school qualification – but failed.

We have an extended conversation about how they make ends meet, what their days look like, what they do when they are bored, what makes them happy and what makes them angry. We talk about corruption and how this affects their chances of finding a job, how they tried starting a business and failed, how they could kill to survive, and more about gambling. My first visit to Katlehong allows me to dive right into the lives of unemployed young South Africans.

## Smell in Thokoza

There is a smell so strong that it makes my nose itch as I exit the car. I park on a bumpy stretch of ground used as a makeshift parking lot, not far from some taxis. These are white, old, dented, and scratched, and certainly not roadworthy, minibuses. Taxi drivers awaiting passengers eat, drink, or fix their cars. No one seems to care about the litter they drop to the ground. This explains that smell.

Lucky is my friend and my guide in Thokoza, another township in the city of Ekurhuleni. He leads the way as we walk across the informal parking lot towards the tin shacks. We pass a central water well. The shacks do not have any fresh water, nor wastewater access. The well is the only water source in the neighbourhood. There is a small stream running slightly downhill, gathering water into a puddle. The water comes from spillage. It is used water from washing and smells like it may contain more abrasive sewage.

A couple of people make the pilgrimage to the water fountain. All of them are women. They do not look young, they do not look old, and their faces have stubborn expressions. They are moving slowly, one woman dragging her feet on the dusty ground, causing a little cloud of dirt particles, which a slight breeze carries away. The women carry containers to fill with the water. They are plastic and appear to hold up to 10 litres of water. Most women carry three of these, one balancing on their heads, and two in each hand. They are not chatty and they seem to limit themselves to the necessary conversation.

We follow an alley between the shacks in which people live. The shacks are fenced off using wooden poles, most of them crooked and connected with strings or netting wire, which create a private area around the tin buildings, and giving the illusion of privacy and ownership. Technically, the land is illegally occupied and the residents do not own title deeds.

We reach the residence of Zodwa, who is the regional branch chair of one of the political parties. That is how Lucky knows her. We are expected. She welcomes us politely, but shyly. We are invited to take a seat on a box in front of her hut. Her accommodation is dark inside, without windows. The only light that falls into the house is through the open entrance door, unveiling one room with a kitchen cabinet and a cooker. A mattress is set up on the opposite wall. The small, fenced garden in which we take a seat is mostly brown hard soil. Cardboard covers several patches of the garden. In between these, there is litter. I wonder why someone who does not appear to be too busy would not maintain their garden and pick up the litter. Zodwa offers Lucky the chance to meet an unemployed young neighbour to talk to us. Zodwa herself is also unemployed but falls outside the youth age range of the study.

She briefly disappears, and brings back a man dressed in blue overalls, who introduces himself as Xolani. He is even shyer than Zodwa. He looks to the ground when he talks, and constantly avoids eye contact. His English is basic, and he speaks slowly, sometimes searching for his words. He, however, is willing to answer questions. We sit down. Xolani is 30 years old. He moved here from Bergville, a small town at the foot of the Drakensberg mountain range in the province of KwaZulu-Natal. In Thokoza, he rents his shack for R200 a month. He has his matric certificate. The money he makes is from occasional loading and off-loading of trucks. A friend sometimes gives him money when he is short on his rent.

We have a brief conversation. Lucky occasionally helps to translate between Zulu and English and at the end we agree to meet again. He

*Figure 1.3* Impressions from the field – Thokoza.
Source: Author's photos.

promises to bring many friends so they can share their stories with me. He hopes that their voices are being heard to improve their lives.

## Hope in Knysna

The red light in the fuel gauge is shining brightly. We are on the last drop of fuel as we climb up the hills outside the town of Knysna on South Africa's southern coast in an old Ford Fiesta. The ups and downs lead past different areas. We go first through shacks adorned with colourful paintings depicting the businesses they house, then monotonous identical government low-cost houses (known in South Africa as Reconstruction and Development Programme or RDP houses), past a gated community of shacks housing the local Rastafari community, then further up the hills, where there are mostly untidy shacks.

The people we pass – children and elderly adults, either black or of coloured – look at us driving past them. Most turn their heads to follow us, their expressions a mix of curiosity and uncertainty. We are clearly outsiders, intruders, or so it felt to me.

Malcolm, our guide, explains the areas as we pass them, and describes who lives in each place. Malcolm would be considered to be coloured, but he does not like to be called coloured. He prefers being described as brown, as he trails his heritage back to the Khoisan, the autochthon population of South Africa, who were called Bushmen by white settlers. The Khoisan were displaced by black communities coming from the North. Today, the Khoisan language is not even recognised as one of South Africa's 11 official languages. Malcolm runs vegetable stores at the local market, which he later proudly shows us.

He runs a community project for the most disadvantaged youths in the area. The youth collect trash in the area and sell it to recyclers. With the proceeds, Malcolm finances a community centre, where young people have internet access and are trained to use the world-wide web. At least that is his plan. He promises to show us how far he has got with it and to take me there, deep into the township, far up the hills.

We stop, and I am astonished. The view from where we parked the car is breath-taking. We overlook the Knysna lagoon from a vantage point far above the sea. The islands in the lagoon, the mountains in the background, and the clear air with soft clouds floating over the mountain range that separates the lagoon from the sea are a uniquely placid sight.

We are in the middle of the Knysna Township, which is probably the South African township with the best view. Around us are low-income homes, with some RDP houses, some metal shacks, and some wooden shacks.

We arrive at a container which has been created into a community centre, with its IT training facility, and a recycling hub-to-be. The container is painted colourfully to depict recyclable items such as cardboard boxes, a plastic bottle, or a metal tin can, which are humanised with faces, eyes, mouths, arms, and legs. The container is surrounded by actual waste: cardboard, plastic bottles, and tin cans. The recycling element of the project has apparently not started yet. Malcolm unlocks the heavy padlock on the container doors. The inside is dark and empty. The funding is missing to kick off the project.

We attract attention, and a few children gather around the container and ourselves. They keep their distance, sit down and observe. It is a Wednesday morning, and I wonder why they are not at school.

## Help in Langa

As a woman passes the gate and walks towards the entrance door, she speaks in the vernacular (a local South African language) loudly, as if she was behind a church pulpit. Her voice carries life experience, and confidence. The residents of the house peek out of the door and see Sister Winnie leading a small group of black women, a coloured man, and white men and women towards the house.

Sister Winnie is a nurse, who retired from her job at a government hospital, and now works in the community health service of the Order of St John. She is rather short, and strongly built. Her hair is covered by a headscarf. Her face looks friendly but determined. She has an aura of authority, despite her petite physique. The black women, who are much younger, are community health workers. The community healthcare programme she runs is an initiative of the City of Cape Town and provides home care for elderly and frail people who do not have health insurance.

I am invited to follow the community healthcare volunteers to a few households in which they take care of the elderly. This is how I gain insights into healthcare and how these volunteers give their best to take care for the elderly and sick in their community.

I am greeted shyly, but with respect. We stand in a dark room with a bed. Every room, however, seems to be a bedroom for someone. The rooms are filled with a lot of furniture, wide couches, tall shelves, big tables, and many boxes. The darkness and the minimal space create a heavy mood. Sister Winnie explains what they do and how they organise themselves to help the community most effectively, particularly the sick and elderly.

The singing we do before entering, I learn later, is a sign of respect; an announcement of guests. This ensures the hosts that we post no threat to them. The fear of home invasions by strangers is common in the Cape Flats, where Langa is situated. It is an area known colloquially as the killing fields because the murder rate is the highest in the country. Children routinely get abducted and raped, and nearly every household is affected by at least one crime per year. Community health workers such as Sister Winnie are only dispatched to work in their own neighbourhoods where they are known by others, and where they are familiar with the terrain.

# Reference

Grill, B., (2018). *Mit Soldaten gegen Gangster: Neuer Bürgermeister von Kapstadt.* Retrieved from www.spiegel.de/forum/politik/neuer-buergermeis ter-von-kapstadt-mit-soldaten-gegen-gangster-thread-821934-1.html
Expert interviews
Participating observations

# 2  Methodology

## The path to building scenarios

This chapter explains the methodological foundations of this book: why we use scenarios, how they are built and which underlying information is fed into them. If you are less interested in the how but are more curious about the what, skip this chapter.

Youth employment scenarios in South Africa are a novelty in three ways. Firstly, youth (un)employment, although the country's most pressing mid-term issue, has not been researched holistically in a way that enables a fundamental understanding of the issues and crafting of sustainable solutions. Secondly, ethnography has not been the methodology of choice for scenario planners to understand the context and path dependency that is required to derive scenarios for and illustrate future states. Thirdly, the framework developed for understanding youth employment for this book is universal and can be applied in any country to understand the dynamics of its youth.

Economists and anthropologists are not aligned on the validity of each other's research. Economists believe in a large number of data points that can be statistically evaluated, while anthropologists trust in the deep insights drawn from spending time with a limited number of individuals. As a result, economists often struggle with issues of validity, and anthropologists for representativeness. This clash of quantitative and qualitative research can be harmonised in a complex system view by quantitatively understanding the magnitude of the challenge and qualitatively understanding the context of it.

This book aims to provide a holistic overview of the situation of youth employment in South Africa today and what it is likely to be by 2040. All themes and elements deemed to be relevant to the research were addressed, although the depth varied depending on their relevance to the overall picture.

DOI: 10.4324/9781003186052-3

The world cannot be understood without numbers. But the world cannot be understood with numbers alone.

Along the lines of Hans Rosling's philosophy of Factfulness, which debunks common perceptions of data, this book relies on quantitative and qualitative data to draw a picture that is as close to reality as possible. These sources include:

- Field research in 26 municipalities with the highest youth unemployment in South Africa in absolute terms.
- Ninety interviews with topic experts across several fields relating to youth employment and a scenario "sounding board" consisting of 27 experts, ranging from teachers, social workers, academics, business representatives, and policy makers to affected youth.
- Statistical analyses of employment data.

Combining these sources leads to:

- Building of the scenarios for 2040.
- Recommendations on how to tackle youth unemployment in today's South African socioeconomic environment.

## Field research across South Africa

Independent field research was conducted in areas with mostly disadvantaged backgrounds, namely the townships of Katlehong, KwaThema, and Thokoza in Gauteng, and Langa, Nyanga, and Knysna in the Western Cape. This book also contains insights from field research that was conducted in collaboration with the Centre for Development and Enterprise (CDE), a South African public policy research and advocacy organisation.

As locations for this research, the 20 municipalities with the highest absolute youth unemployment were selected. These are Buffalo City (East London), Bushbuckridge (Mpumalanga Province), Cape Town, Emalahleni (Witbank), Emfuleni ( Vereeniging), Ekurhuleni (East Rand), eThekwini (Durban), Greater Tubatse (Burgersfort), Johannesburg, Madibeng (Brits), Makhado (Louis Trichardt), Mangaung (Bloemfontein), Matjhabeng (Welkom), Mbombela (Nelspruit), Msunduzi (Pietermaritzburg), Nelson Mandela Bay (Qqeberha, formerly Port Elizabeth), Polokwane (Pietersburg), Rustenburg, Thulamela (Thohoyandou), and Tshwane (Pretoria) (see Figure 2.1).

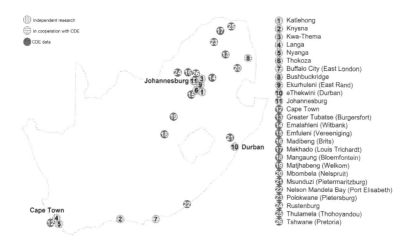

*Figure 2.1* Field research locations.
Source: Author's illustration.

The field research contained ethnographic elements such as participant and environment observations, key informant interviewing, and gathering of cases, but it was not a longitudinal full ethnography.

In many of my interactions with young people, I was often met with curiosity but not with hostility or made to feel unwelcome. Even those who were a bit shy wanted to speak and share their experiences and perspectives. This gave the research a depth beyond the statistics.

Questions used that evoked enthusiastic and insightful responses included:

- What do you do for a living?
- What does a typical day look like for you?
- I often hear that South African youths are lazy… do you think that is true?
- What are the challenges you face when looking for a job?
- Who do you look up to and why?
- What makes you angry?
- What makes you happy?
- What do you want to know about the future?

Being a foreigner from another continent appeared to be a distinct advantage in approaching and talking to young South Africans. Coming from a country with no colonial baggage in South Africa helped to create an impression that I was not approaching the youth with existing prejudices and preconceptions about their situation.

This allowed me to tap into the experiences of the interviewees in an environment of trust. I could also share my own experiences and learnings. Accessing the personal stories and feelings of people is a long way from the analytical and data-driven world of consulting I am used to. The research allowed me to apply a mixed methods approach to gather practical insights into the issues.

## Learning from experts

This book utilises three forms of expert interactions: Expert interviews, an expert sounding board, or a Scenario Board. In total, 90 interactions took place with 76 experts in 90 interviews and presentations. Additionally, two Scenario Board discussions were held to discuss the findings.

The interviewees covered the disciplines of politics, policymaking, business, and non-profit organisations working with the youth. To decrease bias and to receive feedback on the research, a Scenario Board was established bringing 17 experts together as a panel for discourse. This was a group of people selected for their expertise in their area of specialisation across all the disciplines covered in the 90 interviews. This setting allowed the research findings to be challenged, as well as each other's opinions. The panellists were selected based on previous interviews, their depth of relevant expertise, and availability.

## Understanding data

Statistical data provides the foundation for building scenarios. Visualised data explains the status quo of the youth employment situation in South Africa, illustrating employment status differentiated according to age, gender, ethnicity, education, urban and rural areas, provinces, formality, as well as its development over time.

In order to produce a reliable frame to hang the scenarios on, the quality of data needs to be sufficiently comprehensive. South Africa has a reliable statistics institution, Statistics South Africa (StatsSA), as well as several think tanks that provide in-depth data, such as the South African Institute of Race Relations (IRR). Further to this, the World Bank's database (World DataBank), Gapminder, the Economist, and the United Nations provide aggregated additional socio-economic data.

## Building scenarios

Everyone is keen to look into the future. There are two elementary ways to do so: firstly by extrapolating the known and secondly by considering the extremes of possible events. The first method is making a prognosis or forecasting, while the second is scenario analysis.

"When a butterfly flaps its wings on one side of the world, it could cause a storm on the other side." This metaphor, known as the butterfly effect, explains why the prognosis method does not always work, but why extreme situations can only be covered by scenarios.

Imagine leaving the house. It is sunny. Three hours later, you come back completely soaked. You did not expect any rain based on the weather you observed before you left. You made the mistake of expecting the weather to stay as it was.

You can be more advanced, and check the weather forecast, which might trigger you to take a jacket or an umbrella. You would be relying on someone else's forecast, who is an expert and who has access to better techniques. The weather forecast is very accurate, even over a period of time.

But what happens if you travel? Imagine you fly to Cape Town. You check the weather forecast. Let's assume it forecasts rain and a temperature of 17 degrees Celsius. You are likely to wear something warm, like a sweater, and bring something to guard against the rain, such as an umbrella.

If you are staying for a week or more, the forecast will give you an idea of what else to pack. You decide on shorts and a shirt for the sunny and dry days.

Now, imagine you are planning a trip to another country. You will be there for more than 10 days. So, you do not have any weather forecast indicating how you should pack. You ask a friend who is in Cape Town and she tells you it is sunny now, there is nothing to worry about. However, you do not want to end up soaked and ask another friend who travels to Cape Town regularly. She tells you that Cape Town can have four seasons in a day. It can be hot or cold and dry or wet any time. You now know that you should pack for: dry and cold weather, dry and hot weather, hot and wet, and cold and wet weather. You have just done a scenario analysis (see Figure 2.2).

Scenario analysis, compared to a prognosis approach, does not rely on historical data to draw an accurate picture of a single scenario in the future, but takes a broad view to show several alternative future worlds that require a change of past direction to get to.

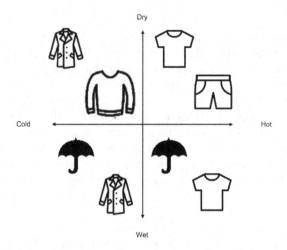

*Figure 2.2* No forecast packing list.
Source: Author's illustration.

Scenarios describe possible future states, including the pathway towards them. They do not predict the future but allow for critical developments and factors to be highlighted in order to draw attention to essential drivers of a future condition.

This means they can be used for a variety of applications, ranging from macro-economic developments of nations to product introductions by companies.

One of the most famous scenarios in the African context is Clem Sunter's discussion on the likely state of South Africa in the post-apartheid era. The scenarios were contained in a book published in 1987 called *The World and South Africa in the 1990s* based on the research drawn up by a scenario team put together by his then employer, mining giant Anglo American.

Scenario methodology allows for: generating knowledge on the status quo and the possible future status of countries or organisations, among other entities. This is done by discussing potential developments with experts and combining different opinions to produce scenarios that outline future threats and opportunities.

Scenario analysis follows four significant phases. The first phase is the determination of the scenario field targets, asking precise questions to adequately survey the subject of the study. Ideally, scenarios have a clear scope regarding the topic, geography, and time. The second phase involves the identification and collection of key factors – the major factors that can influence future developments.

In phase three, analysis of the key factors illustrates the variety of possible developments of each scenario. In phase four – the generation of the scenarios – all the information is collated to build specific scenarios. A fifth additional phase is "scenario implications." This involves drawing up strategies to either achieve a scenario or devising mitigation strategies to tackle a scenario.

Sunter was successful in triggering discussions on a political, economic, and social level, which shows the impact scenarios can have on public discourse and analysis.

Scenario planning has been used in South Africa over the past decades to understand how the country could possibly develop. Sunter pioneered scenarios on South Africa, with a view to shedding light on the political transition from the oppressive apartheid regime to a post-apartheid government.

In 1987, when he published the scenarios in the book *The World and South Africa*, the country's position in the world and the global perceptions of the country were very different from modern South Africa. The international community pursued a policy of isolation and sanctions against the apartheid regime, including former colonial powers, which was lifted after the country became democratic.

Sunter derived two scenarios for South Africa based on the possible interactions between the actors: the High Road and the Low Road. The High Road involved minimal sanctions, small government, decentralised power, and joint negotiation, while the Low Road predicted the opposite – increased sanctions, a controlled economy, a centralised government, and eventual confrontation and conflict.

Several scenario analyses on South Africa followed. The Mont Fleur Scenarios, named after the farm in the Cape winelands at which they were developed, were published in 1992, in the middle of South Africa's political transition from apartheid. The scenarios were named after birds and a winged mythical figure, alluding to their flying capabilities. They aimed to understand the path through the negotiated political transition by drawing up four scenarios, using a stepwise approach.

The Ostrich was the result of a failure to negotiate a settlement. The Lame Duck scenario examined the outcomes of a slow and indecisive transition following successful negotiations. If the transition was bold and decisive, but the government's policies were not sustainable, this would be the Icarus scenario. Lastly, if all of the intersections were followed along the positive "yes"' path, the Flight of the Flamingos scenario would apply. The following excerpts provide more detail of these respective scenarios.

In 2009, the Dinokeng scenarios were drawn up, named after the game farm Dinokeng near Pretoria, which examined the likely state of South Africa by 2020. This 2009 research also draws a two-by-two matrix to illustrate its three scenarios. However, the matrix is based on the analysis of three main situations: the status quo, answering the question "where are we today?" as well as looking at the country's accomplishments, and barriers.

The categories analysing achievements and challenges cover the five drivers, namely politics, the economy, social status, education, and health. The axes of the derived matrices are the "character of civil society," ranging from engaged to disengaged on the $y$-axis, and "capacity of the state," ranging from effective to ineffective. The three scenarios are walk together (engaged and effective), walk behind (disengaged and effective), and walk apart (disengaged and ineffective).

South African academic and writer Frans Cronje published two sets of scenarios in the book trilogy known as the *Time Traveller's Guide* series. The first book in the series, published in 2014, outlines scenarios for South Africa in 2024. The second set, published three years later in 2017, interprets the possible reality and status of South Africa by 2030.

The first alludes to Sunter's road metaphors. Cronje identifies five key drivers, which he calls highways. They are: (1) the future of the ruling party, (2) citizens' ability to change the government, (3) the future of the South African government, (4) the capability of the state to continue social welfare, and (5) economic policy.

He identifies economic development and the citizen's ability to change the government (give feedback) as the two key drivers, which related to four scenarios: (1) the narrow road (good economy but weak feedback mechanisms), (2) the wide road (good economy and good feedback mechanisms), (3) the toll road (good feedback mechanisms but weakened economy), and (4) the rocky road (weak feedback mechanism and weak economy).

In Cronje's 2030 scenarios, he finds meeting popular expectations, ranging from unmet to met expectations, as the most uncertain driver. The role of the state, ranging from dominant state to weak state, is viewed as the most impactful driver. This spans the four scenarios: (1) rise of the right (dominant state and popular expectations met), (2) rise of the rainbow (weak state and expectations met), (3) the break-up (weak state and expectations unmet), and (4) tyranny of the left (dominant state and unmet expectations).

South African academic and founder of the Institute of Security Studies, Jakkie Cilliers, painted three scenarios for the South Africa of 2034. Cilliers did not build on driving forces forming a scenario matrix but made short-term predictions about the 2019 elections and what effects the outcome could have on the country's trajectory. This includes a prognosis based on exact results for the elections in 2019, 2024, and 2029. Three scenarios are Bafana Bafana, Nation Divided, and Mandela Magic.

The most recent example of scenarios on South Africa is the Indlulamithi, the "giraffe looking above the trees" scenarios, published in 2018 and looking at South Africa in 2030. The researchers identified three key driving forces: social inequity; resistance, resentment, and reconciliation; as well as institutional and leadership capacity. They came up with three scenarios: iSbhujwa, an enclave bourgeois nation; Nayi le Walk, a nation in step with itself; and Gwara Gwara, a floundering, false dawn.

There have been similar approaches for understanding the future of youth in Africa. The Kenyan Youth Scenarios were published in 2011, looking forward 19 years ahead to 2030. They are a lucid example of how scenario planning can be applied in the African context, highlighting the dynamics that having a large young population as a percentage of the total creates.

This research applies the same methodology as that used in Kenya – identifying drivers, ranking them according to impact and uncertainty, and describing the four scenarios spanned by a two-by-two matrix. The researchers in that study investigated the drivers by provinces before aggregating them into a national scenario.

The most impactful driver was identified as participation and the most uncertain driver as equality. They selected water as their guiding theme, resulting in four scenarios: the Tsunami scenario (active participation and inequality); the Ocean scenario (active participation and equality); the Waterfall scenario (passive participation and equality); and the Pond scenario (passive participation and inequality).

## Scenario methodology

Scenario analysis is the chosen instrument for this book to describe the possible future for South Africa by 2040 in light of its youth employment challenge. The model chosen to develop the youth employment scenarios for 2040 in this research aligns with Cronje's work on South African scenarios that project forward to 2024 and 2030.

The work on youth employment follows four major steps.

The first is establishing an understanding of the status quo of youth employment in South Africa, using statistical and contextual data, as done in the field research, along with the expert interviews, and thorough analysis of StatsSA data. The second step is identifying the drivers and underlying forces that determine the development of youth employment in South Africa.

The third step is to rank the drivers by impact, and levels of uncertainty. Based on the lived experience of the expert panel, the expert participants discuss and decide on the relative importance of the employment drivers. The result is a ranking of all drivers based on their impact on youth employment and the uncertainty of their occurrence.

The fourth and final step is to create a two-by-two four-field matrix and design the four scenarios. The most impactful and the most uncertain divers are selected as axes for the matrix. The most impactful driver is drawn as the *y*-axis of the matrix, and the most uncertain driver is plotted as the *x*-axis. The positive development of the most impactful driver sits atop the matrix (positive *y*-values), with a negative development on the bottom (negative *y*-values). Similarly, a positive development of the most uncertain driver is found on the right (positive *x*-values) and a negative development on the left (negative *x*-values).

The four resulting fields are where the four scenarios are situated. The two axes delineate a frame. The other drivers that are neither the most uncertain, nor the most impactful, will be considered in the description of the scenarios (refer Figure 2.3).

The scenarios are located at the ends of the axes. Thus, the scenarios illustrate the extreme states in which the topic being examined, in this case youth employment in South Africa by 2040, could be by the target date. The likely scenario for 2040 will be in the area between these four extreme scenarios. This development does not only occur within the two main drivers – most impactful and most uncertain – but also within all supporting drivers that are not illustrated in the two-dimensional matrix.

The scenario in the centre occurs when there is no change of the status quo until 2040, which is unlikely to happen. Also, it therefore contradicts the applied logic to attribute likelihoods to each scenario. Consequently, as the scenarios are not the extrapolated status quo, a regression analysis is not a feasible method (Figure 2.4).

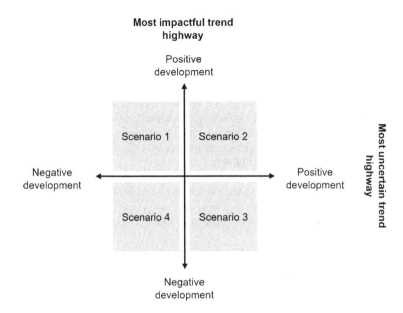

*Figure 2.3* Scenario matrix.
Source: Author's illustration.

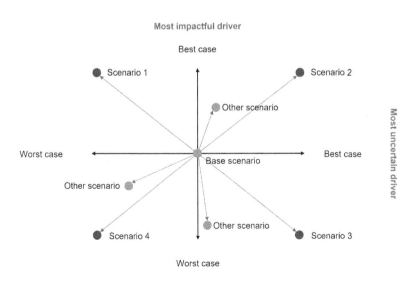

*Figure 2.4* Possible scenarios.

## Bibliography

Altbaker, A., & Bernstein, A. (2017). *No country for young people: The crisis of youth unemployment and what to do about it.* Johannesburg: CDE.

Bernstein, A. (2016). *Jobs: The growth agenda. Priorities for mass employment and inclusion.* Johannesburg: CDE.

Bernstein, A. (2017, April). *Youth employment in South Africa.* Johannesburg.

Business Tech (2018). *This is what South Africa could look like in 2030.* Retrieved from https://businesstech.co.za/news/government/253295/this-is-what-south-africa-could-look-like-in-2030/

Cilliers, J. (2017). *Fate of the nation: Three scenarios for South Africa's future.* Johannesburg: Jonathan Ball Publishers.

Cronje, F. (2013). *Beyond the high road: A scenario analysis of the prospect for political stability in South Africa over the period to 2024* (PhD). North-West University, Potchefstroom.

Cronje, F. (2014). *A time traveller's guide to our next ten years.* Cape Town: NB Publishers.

Cronje, F. (2017). *A time traveller's guide to South Africa in 2030.* Cape Town: Tafelberg.

Geus, A. de (2002). *The living company: Habits for survival in a turbulent business.* Boston, MA: Harvard Business Review Press.

Geus, A. de (2011). *The living company: Growth, learning and longevity in business.* London: Nicholas Brealey Publishing.

Ilbury, C., & Sunter, C. (2001). *The mind of a fox: Scenario planning in action.* Cape Town: Human & Rousseau.

Ilbury, C., & Sunter, C. (2007). *Socrates & the fox: A strategic dialogue.* Cape Town: Human & Rousseau.

Indlulamithi (2018). *Indlulamithi South Africa scenarios 2030: Look above the trees.* [online].

Kahane, A., Le Roux, P., & Maphai, V. (1992). The Mont Fleur scenarios: What will make South Africa be like in the year 2002? *Deeper News, 7*(1), 1–22.

Kosow, H., & Gassner, R. (2008). *Methods of future and scenario analysis: Overview, assessment and selection criteria* (Vol. 39). Bonn: German Development Institute.

Ramaphele, M., Ndungane, N., Menell, R., Maphai, V., Machel, G., & Head, B. (2009). *The Dinokeng scenarios.* [online].

Rosling, H., Rosling, O., & Rönnlund, A. R. (2018). *Factfulness: Ten reasons we're wrong about the world – and why things are better than you think.* New York, NY: Flatiron Books.

Schirmer, S., & Bernstein, A. (2017). *Business, growth and inclusion: Tackling youth unemployment in cities, towns and townships.* Johannesburg: CDE.

Schirmer, S., Steuart, I., & Storme, E. (2017). *Youth unemployment: An agenda for action. How to build constructive business-government relationships in urban areas.* Johannesburg: CDE.

Sunter, C. (1987). *The world and South Africa in the 1990s.* Cape Town: Human & Rousseau.
Van der Merwe, L. (2008). Scenario-based strategy in practice: A framework. *Advances in Developing Human Resources, 10*(2), 216–239.
Expert interviews
Participating observations

# 3    Youth and work in South Africa

This chapter sheds light on the history of labour in South Africa, explains what it takes for South African youth to succeed at finding work, and focuses on how the tough reality of unemployed South Africans struggling to find a job. This chapter makes the daily struggle of South African youth tangible through multiple impressions for the field.

## A brief history of labour

As a result of the country's colonialist-capitalist conquest, traditional institutions in the country shifted. Chiefs became colonial bureaucrats, and the ownership of cattle has become a savings vehicle for the proletarians who are largely dependent on wage labour. Colonialism, Christianity, and capitalism have all transformed the South African socioeconomic sphere. Western influences have transformed the concept of work into a dependency on wage labour.

Traditionally, the head of a household married polygamously, providing a stable social and economic structure. The man, the head of the family, was responsible for cattle herding and his wives and children would farm. Only with the king's permission could a couple get married, involving *ilobolo* or the bride price, where the husband's family pay cattle to the wife's family according to the wife's apparent child-bearing abilities.

The discovery of first diamonds (1867 in Kimberly), then gold (1886 in Johannesburg) resulted in a radical change to the traditional family and work routine, as colonial powers gained interest in this valuable land. In the process, the indigenous people were dispossessed and resettled. Their farming and cattle-rearing activities were affected, and taxes were introduced. Both measures dramatically reduced the families' ability to pay *ilobolo*. The only alternative to raising the funds for *ilobolo* to enable children to marry became wage labour.

DOI: 10.4324/9781003186052-4

As a result, indigenous South Africans were introduced to the concept of migrant wage labour, which mostly meant working in the mines. Young men migrated from settlements to work in mines, often for several months at a time. This labour-induced migration put a strain on marriages. The spread of Christianity reduced the historically prevailing trend of polygamy, and most marriages became monogamous. There was a gradual shift from traditional marriages, which depends on the respective families' wealth, to modern marriage, defined by the capacity and need to work.

Over the decades, wage labour has become part of African manhood, as it enables a man to start a family, to pay *ilobolo*, build a house, and nurture the family. In direct opposition to this stereotype of manhood is the phenomenon of unemployment. Unemployed youth are named *umnqolo*, a term traditionally used for "an unmasculine rural man so timid that he won't even herd cattle." Unemployment thus undermines the notion of traditional manhood and can lead to exclusion from traditional social categories.

## The journey of work

Jeremy Seekings, a Professor of Political Studies and Sociology in South Africa, researched the success the youth has had in its journey to finding work, interviewing young people over several years to draw his conclusions.

He found that 18-year-old youths in South Africa, particularly from less advantaged black and coloured communities, were not very successful in finding jobs despite having high aspirations to work. Half of the men were unemployed five years after his initial interaction with them, and just under half of the women. Most were struggling to find a job, to keep a job, or to find a new one.

Participants said their failure to finish school was a key reason for their struggle, which constitutes a recurring experience of failure. Additionally, disadvantaged youth seem to have an unrealistic view of job opportunities. Those they may get without having completed their matric, such as domestic work, would not be paid what they expected which, in some cases, could act as a disincentive to pursue such a job.

Anecdotally, this research finds that young people would be willing to take any job over being idle. However, narratives around responsibility, morality, respect, and style are often contradictory companions in the individuals' struggle to find their place.

However, Seekings found that white urban South African youths started working after completing secondary school, mostly in parallel to their tertiary education. They were not overly selective in the jobs they chose, premising their journey on an inevitable rags-to-riches trajectory. Many had found work through social family ties, while those without a useful network to lean on were savvy enough to build their own networks through personal engagement, preferring to leverage this network rather than simply sending out curriculum vitaes in their search for work. Some white youths set up their own businesses.

In either case, selling their labour helped them to enter the job market and work their way up. Seekings describes this savviness as "work ethic." However, not much is discussed about the enabling context for the activities and decisions taken by white youths compared to the path endured by young people in black and coloured communities in a country with a long history of apartheid and repression.

## Realities of the youth experience

Given the focus of the research for this book on the areas of highest unemployment in South Africa, much of the content relates to the experiences of people in disadvantaged areas where young people on the fringes of the employment market are found. Many interviews were conducted with people in the townships of South Africa to find out about their experience of actual work, the experience of seeking work, their attitude to jobs, and other issues.

Understanding the issues requires first understanding why the unemployed youth seek work and what they hope employment will do for them. What are the aspirations of young South Africans that drive them and lead them to pursue a job opportunity? The answers to these and other questions speak to a longing for belonging and status. Young people talk a lot about looking for jobs to enable them to support families, build homes in the rural areas, buy a car, and find a wife.

But these long-term goals run alongside the harsh reality that they also need to support and feed themselves in the present.

### Daily hustle

There is a thin line between working and not working. Employment is often a matter of hours or days, not one of months and years. At the lowest level of work – manual jobs that do not require qualifications – someone can work for a day and be unemployed again the very next day, while an unemployed person can be employed just as suddenly, also mostly for short-term work. In this informal set up, there is no contract, no structure, and no security, but it serves one key need – that of finding an immediate income. Consequently, looking for a job is a daily routine and a daily hustle.

The routine involves going early in the morning to hubs where people or companies hire people. This could be a traffic intersection, an industrial cluster, or at a factory. Potential jobs may include construction, housekeeping, and sometimes collecting scrap material for recycling at scrapyards. Said one young man interviewed for the research, "I wake up and start looking for work. I go to the local factories. I take any job."

If the day is unsuccessful, the youth will return home. A day of work can net them R300–R500 but a basic rental in a township dwelling is about R350 a month.

### *What 100 rand buys*

During the research, an opportunity arose to understand how a young unemployed South African would spend R100. Research participants were not paid in principle, but one of them, Xolani, asked for money as he indicated he had not been able to buy food for a few days and had to beg his neighbours for leftovers. This young man received R100. The next time I saw him, he explained what he spent this money on.

Xolani spent the first R100 he received on food, power, and hygiene. He explained that he had spent R70 on paraffin to cook, R10 on soap to be able to wash himself after a long time, and R20 on bread. None of these would help him to find work even though they went some way towards satisfying his immediate personal needs.

The search for a job in South Africa can cost about R500 on average per month, most of which is swallowed up by transport costs.

### *No bribe, no job*

One hurdle young South Africans face on their job hunt is being asked for bribes to have their applications processed. Some applications require entry testing and applicants have to put money inside their answer paper in order to have a chance of passing. If they attempt to write the test without offering the money, they will fail regardless of their test result. Corruption adds another layer of cost in the job-hunting process and the jobless do not have the money to pay bribes.

Another element of corruption in this regard is more political. It involves having the right connections to people, political parties, or even families.

Some interviewees mentioned the example of a fire station opening up in the local area but no one in the community being able to secure a job there. Opportunities went to people with political connections. Such behaviour leads young people to believe that merit is not always a criterion in getting access to jobs and opportunities.

### The dream job

Elevated levels of frustration among the youth often leads them to stop even trying to find an occupation, even though the expectations for a job are low. Asked what their minimum requirement for a job might be, such as the amount of money they would work for, the type of work they would do, and the location, many of the young people interviewed had few or no expectations. They are mentioned only by their first names in this book.

"I'd take any job, even [as] brick layer, plasterer, or plumber," said Themba in an interview in 2017.

> You can spend even the whole month without getting any job, up until maybe here on the location you are asked by the old lady to come and fix her door and then you get R50. At last. You take it. Because you don't have something, you fix the door.

Although having no reservations about the type of job he would accept, Xolani, another young interviewee, has aspirations. "I would like to become a truck driver, but I can't afford the licence of R6,500." Khulejani, Thabale, Nomsa, and Khanyisile said they would like to work in a bakery, or as a security guard.

On the other hand, Sanele and Themba did not have a specific profession in mind, as long as it paid. "Three point five [R3,500] a month, it will be okay. Just for living on, but it is not enough. It is just to maintain," said Themba.

### Role models

Could the reason for the low aspirations of many young South Africans be the result of a lack of role models? Who do they look up to? After some consideration, several people interviewed said they looked up to teachers, policemen, and security guards in their neighbourhood.

Family did not get a mention. Most of the relatives of the youngsters are unemployed. Many of their families live in the rural areas of the Eastern Cape and expect their children living in

Johannesburg to support them with the little money they do make. One of them, Sanele, looks up to his brother, who, he says, "…can support his family, his kids, and me." Khulejani mentions that he looks up to "people with a qualification, a matric for example" and "people who live here that earn money." He mentions policemen and security guards, but says both are corrupt. Xolani says he does not look up to anyone.

Ntokozo from KwaThema reports that those who may qualify as role models because they had made money, had left the township and its misery behind and look back in disgrace, not supporting their former fellow sufferers.

> They think, "I get my money, I'm out of this nonsense." So they all leave. No one stays behind. So, you know there's a guy that lives there in that house, but he doesn't live here. He lives in Sandton and when he comes here, he looks down on us. So, you want to look up to him but when he looks at you, he's like – you know. We are facing it daily. I believe that even if I was to get money, I would actually leave.

That's the culture with our society, when we get money, we leave. We don't want to have anything to do with this place, this godforsaken place. You are going to live in the [wealthy] suburbs with other people, because these ones are going to pull you down. You have this mentality that the township is going to pull you down so it's better for you to leave and grow elsewhere. But if we look at it in a different way, if people like us stayed in the township, we could actually develop it. A lot of young people would have access to us, we could help their dreams to materialise and they would materialise other people's dreams. There are a lot of things that could happen in the township. But when they get their money, they leave.

In Johannesburg, Benjamin and his friends say they do not look up to anyone in their community as there is no one there that has achieved anything that they aspire to. "I did not ask for information from my community because mostly in my community, there is no one who did what I wanted to do."

There are, at best, just a few role models for unemployed youth in their environments. A person's ability to make money is what best positions them to be the person others look up to. But often these role models lack integrity and are corrupt, or they move out of the township and look down on the people they left behind.

### Escaping reality: gambling, alcohol, and drugs

"On the weekends we gamble, and we drink alcohol big time, man, every fucking [sic] weekend. We really want that happiness inside you, to forget the problems just for that moment." Themba and his friends describe how gambling, alcohol, and drugs are used to escape the misery of the everyday life.

Dice games are infamous. Kids start playing them at school, even though gambling is illegal. The rules are easy: two dice, at least two players, and usually a R5 bet per round. The player throws the dice. If the player rolls a 7 or an 11 as a sum of both dice, he wins. If he rolls any other number, he has to roll again until he either rolls the same number as in his first throw, or a 7 or 11. If he rolls the same number again, he wins. If he rolls a 7 or 11, he loses. The attraction lies in the perception of big wins: You can win a lot in one round, and you only lose little per round. Big wins are the dream. Themba talks about someone having won R2000.

While gambling is illegal, it gives the youth an occupation and a passion, preventing them from being exposed to more harmful crimes. The exposure to alcohol, on the other hand, is riskier as it does not require a group setting as gambling does, and thus is independent of timing and setting. "Scarcity of options, that's the main problem," says Themba.

The Katlehong group points to a group of women close by, saying that even though it is only Monday, they have already consumed alcohol.

> Because we don't have something to do, some of us end up drinking. That is the problem. On Monday, Friday seems too far. Tomorrow they start [again], and then on Wednesday until Friday until Monday, they drink. That's why the corruption and abuse is so high. They are abusing alcohol, some are abusing drugs, some are smoking dagga.

They get the money for their activities from hustling.

> It's called *ukukgereza,* they are hustling for anything they can get. They say "I can sell you this hat, hey do you like it? Give me R5 you can have it." So, you give me R5. I go down there and I can sell this t-shirt and I charge R10 for it. Maybe I can afford a beer with that.

Alternatively, the money or goods to sell are acquired through "expropriation." "If you see young girls, like they're carrying R50 and going to the shops. You take that R50," says one of the Katlehong group.

The group in KwaThema says alcohol consumption has become a focus of social engagement in the community because of a lack of alternatives. Even the youth and children join gatherings in the local pub (shebeen) on a Friday and Saturday evening. "The only place in any township where you can find people, particularly in Ekurhuleni, is a place where there's alcohol."

These evenings can quickly descend into violence and crime.

> We are there to show off. My poverty is better than yours, for example. It's a matter of how you're dressed, the kind of alcohol you buy with money that you do not have. So that's the only space where young people actually come together – and it happens all the time. Even grade six kids are there. This is all we know. This is our life,

says one of the group members.

> Some people get hurt, others get raped there, some get shot. Others get things stolen from them. The kids are vulnerable, but they come there anyway because there is no other space to meet. With sports, you come together and build. But sport is not funded, nor is it taken seriously in the township. There is no place or institution in the township where young people come together besides coming together to use alcohol. Even in the libraries now. You go there, it's empty. People don't care anymore. They have just given up. What's the point?

Children are exposed to alcohol early on. On a visit to the Katlehong township three children were observed – a girl of six or seven, holding a baby boy and another boy, aged perhaps three or four, playing in a tin shack. The earth floor is partly covered with a mat and a blanket, on which lie a smartphone, a doll, and a rake. There is an empty bottle of gin, a cheap brand usually found at the counter of liquor shops, carelessly placed on the glassless window frame. The older boy leans over a 350-ml beer can and a 750-ml beer bottle that lie next to the blanket. Their parents sit outside the shack on white plastic chairs. They claim to be strict Muslims.

Besides the exposure of the youth to alcohol, drugs also appear early in the life of young people in townships. "[There] are those people coming from other worlds. They are killing our society, they are killing our children, they are selling Nyaope to them," said one youngster.

Nyaope is a cocktail of drugs that its users smoke. It is highly addictive and dangerous, particularly for children. The cocktail is a combination of cannabis and heroin with Tenofovir, Emtricitabine, and Efavirenz, all three antiviral drugs used for HIV treatment, which cause an LSD-like psychedelic effect. It also includes Strychnine, Brodifacoum (both pesticides and rat poison), and birth control pills. The amounts of these different components in the drugs tends to be random. Addicts typically smoke Nyaope every four hours.

The Katlehong group points out a man walking slowly by. They claim he is visibly impaired by the pills he takes, for which he pays by collecting bottles for recycling.

> You see one of these guys – this guy is a young man. He's staying here. Look at him. You see now he's collecting the bottle so that he can get that R10 in the scrapyard to go and buy this. It's R12.50 for the half and R25 for the full drug.

Being robbed, raped, or murdered in townships is a daily reality, as is being affected by alcohol and drug abuse. Suicide is another reality as people find a way to end the misery of their lives. One young man says Ntokozo, "It's my brother, he killed himself because he was trying to be happy inside and he decided to use drugs." A young woman in the same group adds,

> People are actually killing themselves now, young people. It's not something we used to find in the township, where a young person of 22 or 23 would be found dead after they hanged themselves. But now it's something we see on a weekly basis. You know the pressure got to them and they couldn't handle it anymore.

The cause of the desperation that can result in suicide is "social pressure." Says a member of the group,

> They think everyone's winning and they ask, "what's happening with me, what's wrong with me?" The pressure of saying time is ticking, what's happening with you? You're getting old, you're supposed to take responsibility, you're supposed to be taking care of yourself. You can't be asking me for money. You know what I mean. Those pressures.

*Crime as a profession: What it takes to make R1,000*

Crime can have several causes and effects, ranging from the need to put food on the table and helping the family to financing drug addiction, which can lead to petty crime, robbery, rape, and murder. As work opportunities are not accessible to many, crime can become a means of survival.

Themba and his friends share an anecdote about young people who have made robbery their profession. They get up early to go to work and make money, like an employed person.

> In the morning you stand on the corner waiting for those who are going to work, take their phones, take their money, take some stuff, and you sell it. It's not that you are too lazy to go to work, to get job, but we don't get the jobs. If you can rob a person at four o'clock in the morning when you are rushing for the first train at twenty past four, that person is not lazy because he's waking up early so he can grab people that are going for the first train. If that person can't get a job, he's going to wake up early in the morning and go to "work."

Besides robbing fellow township neighbours, who own little more than the robber, there seems to be an even more radical possibility to earn money. The Katlehong group talks about contract killings. A murder is worth R1,000 – big money in this community.

> That's why in the location [Katlehong] you find that most youth end up killing people because those who have money come with one thousand [rand]. You don't have money, and it's around the month end so you need money. We are told "You can shoot this guy for me – it's easy to do that because you don't have job." But it's not that we are lazy.

Besides robbery and murder, there are many other ways to acquire money illegally. In KwaThema, another township south-east of Johannesburg, the story of the illegal miner is told by Ntokozo's group. Illegal mining, undertaken by men known locally as *zama zama*, is common in the old mine dumps and tunnels around the former mining town of Johannesburg.

The Witwatersrand, which is home to Johannesburg, commonly referred to as the City of Gold because of its long mining history. It is home to many closed gold mines that have been hijacked by gangs who allow access to miners in exchange for a share of the excavated goods.

Safety measures are non-existent and miners risk their lives on a daily basis to dig for treasure. "They go to an abandoned mine and just go down. You mine whatever you can mine and then you come out with what you have."

### Spiritual support but no money

The role of the church and religion seems to vary greatly among young South Africans. Church communities are seen by many as a provider of actual and spiritual opportunities, which means people continue to go to church in the hope of being offered an opportunity.

A young woman in Ekurhuleni shared her reasons for working as an usher at a church without payment. She recounted, "I organise everything up to cleaning the toilets to get some recognition for it." Although the recognition is not forthcoming, she continues with the job because,

> We still work our day, we go to those offices with the best smile, and dress our best with God's grace and that is why we are here today, even, to have a voice, to say we are employed. We still have that, and we still dream.

But many others are critical of the role of the church. The group around Ntokozo used to visit a Methodist church regularly, but not anymore. One woman shared her views.

> There's no food and stuff like that, so the young people are just done with that. Our education taught us that we must not identify with the church. We know better than our parents. To be honest, a lot of young people know that the church represents something that we're not. So, a lot of people will forego the opportunities that come with the church on the principle that "I'm not Christian and I know that Christianity was brought into my country to oppress me."
>
> Just because you are impoverished doesn't mean that you are stupid. We are also educated. We are revolutionaries. We're putting our foot down and saying we're not going. Politics teaches that the church was brought to Africa to colonise our people. We understand that Christianity is not us, it broke our families apart, it changed the way we live by teaching us about a God that we don't know. We are educated, we know these things, we can explain in an anthropological sense.
>
> The church is a place where we are being taught to perpetuate our poverty and our problems. Even if they have programmes, we

don't want the church programmes and we are not going. I will take [a job offered by the church] because I'm being opportunistic now, but in principle I will not identify with the church and a lot of people are like me in the township. Things have changed,

the young woman said.

It's not like the '70s, when a lot of young people went to the church to be hostesses and hosts. No, it's not like that anymore. We are more liberal and liberated, we are educated now. It's just the poverty aspect of our lives that is putting us down, and we view the church as one of those things that presses us down. This is where you get a lot of judgement. People are supposed to come with you, help you grow. But they look down on you, look down on your family, look down on your mother, look down on your father. People look down at the status of your family when you come to church. They look at how well you dress, how well you speak English. Are you friends with the pastor's children or not? So, it's those things.

This woman says she has been politically active her whole life, first in the Pan-African Congress (PAC), a national Africanist South African political party, and later in the ruling African National Congress (ANC).

Even the youth that choose not to go to church admit that it provides opportunities, whereas those that go do so for spiritual purposes or see their involvement as a contribution to their community.

### Party politics and job opportunities

Does affiliation to a political party in South Africa help people to find jobs? South Africa has a reputation for nepotism, or jobs for pals. The ruling ANC, in particular, is regularly accused of putting friends and family in jobs in a process commonly known as cadre deployment. This practice reaches up to the highest levels, including ministers. There is a belief that the party association may benefit even supporters at the lowest levels in terms of getting employment. Is this really the case?

A politician from KwaThema says,

I don't have a job and I'm part of the ANC. You get deployed by the party without compensation. Let me tell you something about the township. A lot of people in the ANC are people who are not even qualified. Qualified people are complaining at home. If you are not a comrade, you're at home. There are a lot of comrades in the ANC without work and when limited opportunities come, the first person we are going to consider are comrades.

Themba's group experiences the other perspective, which is not being affiliated to a political party. Access to jobs, they claim, lacks transparency and is unfair. Said one, "There is a new fire station here. No one in the community got hired there – only people from somewhere else who know someone in the party."

Party affiliation, at least to card-carrying members of the ANC, does appear to have a positive impact on job opportunities. But being active in a political party has other benefits too. For example, it seems to provide structure in the daily life of the unemployed, as well as a sense of belonging and purpose.

### *The movers versus the stayers*

In South Africa, residential geographies can be differentiated along rural and urban lines. The different categorisations in urban areas include (typically wealthy) suburbs, city centres or central business districts (CBDs), and (typically disadvantaged) townships.

As identified earlier, youth unemployment in rural areas is higher than it is in urban areas, driving the youth to metropolitan centres where they typically end up staying in a township where they have family, friends, as well as others from their home area and ethnicity, and cheap accommodation.

This raises the question of whether the unemployment situation for youth who have moved from a rural area to an urban township is different from that of youths who have grown up in the township. People interviewed represented both categories.

The participants in Katlehong (Themba and his friends) and Thokoza (Khulejani and his friends) moved to the township (the "movers"), whereas the participants in KwaThema (Ntokozo and his friends), Knysna (Adams), Langa, and Nyanga (Winnie) grew up in the township where they lived (the "stayers").

Sihle, a stayer, said she has access to her mother's car for transport, although she needs to cover the expenses for using it. Interviewees in Langa and Nyanga in the Cape were mostly volunteers receiving a stipend of R1,800–R2,200 per month for serving their community, making them technically unemployed. All the stayers mentioned having some kind of support from their families, such as accommodation, free meals, pocket money, or access to job opportunities through their family networks.

The movers, however, do not have that support. Those in this group not only have to find accommodation and food, but they are also expected to support their families in the rural areas. They also do not have networks that could help them to get a job.

This indicates that youth growing up in townships and suburbs are advantaged over those that migrated from their rural home to a township, with the former benefiting from access to local networks and social structures.

### Burning cars gets attention

All participants in the study were asked what makes them happy and angry.

Xolani aspires to being recognised as a happy person. His play to "fix myself" or "uplift my home in KwaZulu-Natal" add to his aspiration to "have money to be like other people." All this, however, requires him to have a job.

The Themba group mentions that drinking alcohol is a way to be happy as it allows them to escape reality. Says one of them, "We drink big time man, every fucking weekend. We really want that happiness inside us." They explain that they are "always thinking about problems and drink just to forget, just for that piece of moment." They drink and gamble to escape their desperate reality and have a little fun. The same group also highlights the joy they have from gambling, which reflects in their excitement as they talk about their upcoming plans to do so.

Other drivers for happiness were to "live a life with a future" or "my family and kids." The response to this question was quite general but the replies to the question of what made them angry were much more specific. The anger is real, while feelings of happiness are much more intangible and even far in the future.

Causes for anger included, "that I have to go so far to find work," "when I vote still nothing changes," "corruption," and "if I don't have money, I can't get a job." Being insulted was also raised. One young man mentions embarrassment, saying that without a job and an income he cannot wash himself, he has to ask for food donations, and he is hungry when he does get an interview for work.

Themba's group members vividly describe their frustrations. One is with public toilets in Katlehong, which the municipality fails to clean for weeks. Destructive protest seems to be their only hope of being heard.

> [We] burn the tires, we do some *toyi-toyi* [protest] and you burn the car and then they'll come to fix it. You see they don't care, so we need to be violent to get their attention. When we are tired, we will end up closing this road and then burn their cars.

### Taking on the foreigners

One option that is open to all youths is taking the initiative and starting their own businesses to generate income. Indeed, many participants talked about their ventures and business ideas. Four examples are listed below.

*The mielie-meal stand*: The Themba group cites interviewees' experience of the effect of competition on their businesses. Mealie meal is a maize flour used to cook *pap*, the most common staple food in the country and region. In their neighbourhood, Ethiopian mealie-meal vendors used to operate alongside South Africans. The Ethiopians had the edge as they charged a lower price. One resident said the South Africans were selling 12.5 kg of mealie meal for R105 and the Ethiopians for R80. "So, we were running to them, but then we make our homeboys angry and then they go to attack them to chase them away. That's why now you cannot see their shops." By eliminating their competition, the South Africans can artificially maintain their high prices.

*The banana stand*: One participant says he sold bananas for R2.50 and apples for R2, which made him a lot of profit. However, a Zimbabwean woman set up a stand close by and undercut his prices, selling bananas for R2 and apples at half of his price, which forced him to eventually close his business.

Asked why he did not lower his prices to stay competitive, he said the Zimbabweans sourced their goods from a cartel, aggregating their purchasing power. "They share the stock and then they sell so that's why they got low prices. So, I'm going alone to get this bunch of bananas, so I need the profit there."

*The spare parts shack*. A woman entrepreneur in Thokoza set up a spare parts shop in a shack next to the taxi rank. She proudly explained her operations and presented her shop. She sold low-value spare parts for the taxis, as she did not have the funds to buy higher-value parts. She planned to move up the value chain once she had the capital. She was able to live well off her business and save money to expand.

*The muffin business*: In Durban, a woman interviewed spoke about an idea she had for a business, but she had not operationalised it. She wanted to bake and sell muffins in her community. She, however, had neither started the business, nor tested her idea. She was held back by financial fears, thinking she needed a significant amount to start, which she did not have. Challenged to break it down to a specific amount, she said she needed about R150 for ingredients. Further questioning revealed that she had not thought about asking friends and family to help with seed capital for the business with small loans repaid as she sold her stock. She seemed surprised to hear that this was a possibility.

All of these examples, but particularly the last case, highlight that entrepreneurial drive exists but it is constrained by a significant lack of self-confidence and initiative to even start a business or find ways to succeed, especially in the presence of competition.

### *Living in the present*

Asking a person about their expectations for the future highlights their fears and hopes, which is why it was added to the mix in interviewing people for this project.

The questions participants raised were, however, focused very much on the present rather than the future. "When will I find a job?" asked one. "Can you take my number for if you hear something?" said another. "Do you have recommendations about how to get a job?" and "Will my life ever change?"

### *Is it help or a scam?*

What happens if someone in despair stumbles across an opportunity that might help in the job hunt? Sanele reported that he had received a text message from Harambee, which is the largest employment bridging provider in South Africa. A public–private partnership, it coaches unemployed youths on how to find a job. Harambee assesses skill levels, including language skills, CV writing skills, and personal interests in order to guide young people along the path to employment. The SMS offered Sanele free registration for one of those assessments.

Sanele, however, had never heard of Harambee before, and was afraid the text might be a scam, one of the many he had heard about. Consequently, and instead of conducting further research, he ignored the SMS, missing out on the opportunity to learn and engage.

### Bibliography

Honwana, A. M. (2012). Social change. In A. M. Honwana (Ed.), *The time of youth: Work, social change, and politics in Africa* (pp. 139–164). Boulder, CO: Kumarian Press Sterling.

Honwana, A. M., & Boeck, F. d. (2005). *Makers & breakers, made & broken: Children & youth as emerging categories in postcolonial Africa*. Oxford: James Curry.

Hunter, M. (2010). *Love in the time of AIDS: inequality, gender, and rights in South Africa.* Bloomington, IN: Indiana University Press.

Morris, H. (Author) (2014, April 22). *Getting high on HIV medication* [Television broadcast].

Seekings, J. (2012). How young people look for work. In A. Bernstein (Ed.), *Coping with unemployment: Young people's strategies and their policy implications* (pp. 16–19). Johannesburg: CDE.

Expert interviews

Participating observations

# 4 Insights into youth unemployment
## The statistics

To build scenarios, one needs to thoroughly understand the status quo of two aspects: data and context. The data provides measurable insights into the situation. Therefore, it is important to work with reliable primary data sets and not with data that has been processed, as this often only provides a snippet of the whole picture that can be interpreted incorrectly without the big picture. The context described in the previous chapters explains the data, answering the questions of how unemployed youth live and how they understand their challenges.

This chapter focuses on the data, building the construct to analyse statistical data to understand the severity of youth unemployment in South Africa. The underlying data originates from trustworthy sources analysed at the most granular level, mostly based on the quarterly labour force surveys issued by Statistics South Africa (StatsSA).

If you are not interested in the granular assessment, you can read the summary below and skip the rest of this chapter.

The key findings at the time of publication were the following.

- South Africa is the least equal society in the world, reflected across income, wealth, education, and opportunities.
- The share of youth in the overall population decreases proportionally, increasing the need for the employed to economically carry the younger and older generations.
- Women are more affected by unemployment and non-participation in the economy than men.
- Out of the 18- to 34-year-old South Africans that make up the labour force (excluding youth that do not intend to work because of still being in the education system or being ill or parenting, among other reasons), 59 percent are jobless.
- Eighteen percent of South African youth want to work but have given up searching (discouraged job seekers), while 41 percent

DOI: 10.4324/9781003186052-5

search for a job without success (unemployed) and 14 percent are actively looking for a job. Fourteen percent are informally (precariously) employed, and only 27 percent are formally employed.

- Rural areas are more affected by unemployment than urban areas. The highest unemployment rates are in the Eastern Cape, Mpumalanga, Northern Cape, Free State, Limpopo, and North-West provinces. Discouragement is highest in the Northern Cape and Limpopo. The Western Cape has by far the highest employment and lowest desperation rate.
- Black South Africans are worse off than coloured, Indian, and white South Africans.
- The longer youth have stayed in the education system, the higher the probability that they are employed.
- The level of youth entrepreneurship is low, at under 5 percent of the youth labour force.

The profile of the average unemployed South African is a black female, aged between 18 and 24, living in a township close to Johannesburg, who dropped out of school before passing her matric qualification, and who has never worked before. Her (fictional) name is Lesedi. Lesedi will return in 2040 and help us to understand the future.

## Population overview

The quality of statistical information on South Africa is relatively sound, with the main statistics bureau, StatsSA, conducting regular representative surveys. The agency conducts quarterly assessments of employment figures, with aggregated socio-economic data also provided by the South African Institute of Race Relations (IRR), the World Bank's database (World DataBank), Gapminder, the Economist, and the United Nations.

In the diagrams below, the age groups are colour coded: children aged 0–14 are highlighted in light grey, youth aged 15–34 are highlighted in dark grey, and adults aged 35 and older are represented in middle grey.

The South African population was estimated to be about 60 million in 2021 with an average life expectancy of 64.1 years. The country's gross domestic product (GDP) per capita is USD ~5,090 per capita nominally, having decreased from about USD8,000 in 2011. It declined by 15 percent in 2019 and 2020, partly driven by the impact of COVID-19 on work.

The GINI coefficient, describing the inequality of the society on a scale from 0 (totally equal income distribution) to 100 (totally unequal income distribution), ranks South Africa as the worst in the world at 63, highlighting the economic divide between rich and poor. In other words, the South African population is unevenly split into first and third world cohorts. The fact that about 50 percent of households live on social grants underlines this stark divide. In comparison, Germany has a GINI coefficient of 31.9, the USA 41.4, and Norway – one of the most equal societies – 27.6.

The breakdown of the population illustrated below shows South Africa's population pyramid on the left, and the most relevant population data on the right. Of the population, 29 percent are children and 34 percent are considered to be youth (see Figure 4.1).

The pyramid shape is quite typical for an emerging country, where there is a wide base with many children, narrowing at the upper end. The causes for this shape are typically high fertility, low child survival rates, and poor health, leading to low life expectancy.

South Africa sees a bend in the population when people reach their mid-20s, with a decrease in childbirth, which evens out at a population

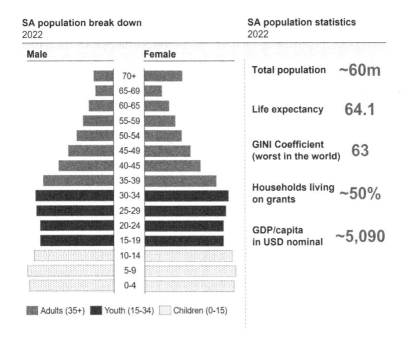

*Figure 4.1* Breakdown of the South African population.

aged about 15. These bends are typical for developing countries, as women start participating in the economy more, moving away from childbearing and domestic work. In South Africa, the end of apartheid in 1994 opened the door for the previously disadvantaged population, mostly blacks, but also coloureds and Indians, to participate more actively in social and economic life.

Today, the country has a fertility rate of ~2.4 children per woman, a child mortality of ~4 percent, and an average life expectancy of 64.1 years.

## Population growth

From 2020 to 2040, the population will have grown by 18 percent on this trajectory. Interestingly, the proportion of adults aged above 35 will increase dramatically from 37 percent in 2015 to 45 percent in 2040, while the proportion of youth and the children decreases, despite being constant in absolute terms. This means that the population growth comes from adults, and not children and youth. Consequently, the population ages and the growth rates decline. This highlights the burden on today's youth to gain access to employment so that they can provide for their parents and their children in the future (Figure 4.2).

Looking at the employment breakdown for the entire South African working-age population, we find only 32 percent employment. About 68 percent of the South African population does not participate in working activities, regardless of whether these activities are formal or informal.

StatsSA defines unemployment as

> persons [...] who: a) were not employed in the reference week, b) actively looked for work or tried to start a business in the four weeks preceding the survey interview, c) were available for work i.e., would have been able to start work or a business in the reference week,

and discouraged as

> a person who was not employed during the reference period, wanted to work, was available to work/start a business, but did not take active steps to find work during the last four weeks, provided that the main reason given for not seeking work was any of the following: no jobs available in the area, unable to find work requiring his/her skills, or lost hope of finding any kind of work.

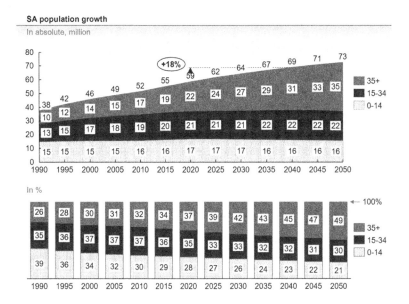

*Figure 4.2* South African population growth.

Both unemployment and discouraged categories are commonly referred to as unemployed.

"Not economically active" refers to, for example, pupils or students or women raising children, or as StatsSA puts it, "Persons aged 15-64 years who are neither employed nor unemployed in the reference week." Out of the 61 percent of the population without a job, 15 percent of the total working-age population are considered to be unemployed, 6 percent are discouraged, and 40 percent are not economically active. About one-third of the unemployed 21 percent has given up looking for a job.

## Employment breakdown

The second part of the illustration shows the split per group by gender (Figure 4.3). The total population has fewer men than women (45 percent vs 55 percent). However, more men are employed than women (52 percent vs 48 percent). Of people without a job, 59 percent are women. This bias against women is represented throughout the chain with women being 52 percent of jobseekers, 60 percent of those

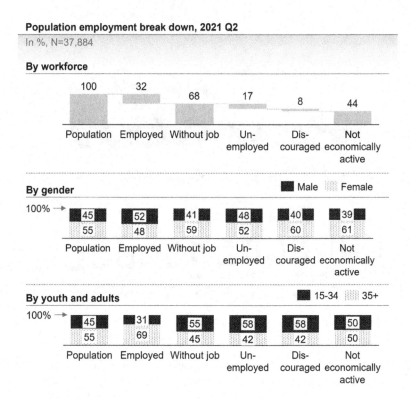

*Figure 4.3* Population employment breakdown.

discouraged from finding work, and 61 percent of those who are not economically active.

The third part of this graphic shows the same split by age group: youth (aged 15–34) versus adults (aged 35+). Although the proportion of the population between youth and adults is about the same (45 percent vs 55 percent), youth are underrepresented in the group of employed people and significantly overrepresented in the group of unemployed. Unemployment and discouragement are associated mostly with youth, representing nearly two-thirds of the total. This is partly because many of them will be still in the education system. Non-economically active youth are mostly still being educated.

Both splits highlight the fact that unemployment in South Africa is statistically a bigger issue for women than it is for men, and a larger issue for youth than for adults.

## Age and gender breakdown

Having established that the youth statistically struggle the most to find employment, the following illustration takes a closer look at the development of the employment status according to age and gender on a normalised scale.

This overview offers several insights into the dynamics of finding a job and into gender differences. For men and women, this perspective allows a split of employment into two subsets, namely: (1) "in education" and "employed" and (2) "discouraged job seeker," "unemployed," and "economically active." Until the age of 19, there is a dynamic happening in which youth "in education" move into all other categories, while "in education" still is the largest category, with a more than 50 percent share.

From the age of 20 upwards, the share of "in education" decreases to less than half, while the sum of the categories of "in education" and "employed" stays more or less constant. Also, the share of "non-active," "unemployed," and "discouraged" remains stable. What does this tell us? Firstly, from the age of 20 years onwards, education tends to be transferred to employment, and secondly, if a person is in any of the categories "non-active," "unemployed," or "discouraged" by the age of 20, the data shows that it does not seem that likely that this person will change his or her category significantly as they grow older (Figure 4.4). The overall shape of the share of categories by age looks similar for men and women. Also, the overall proportion of "in education," "unemployed," and "discouraged" is similar. However, the share of non-activity is about double to triple that from age 21 for women, compared to men. This happens at the cost of employment.

So why is the proportion of non-activity for women so high? Assuming that the male share of economic inactivity is mostly caused by health concerns and applying the same to women, the share for non-active women without health concerns is about one-sixth. This can be explained by pregnancy, and the social bias towards women being expected to take care of a household and children.

## Unemployment and NEET rates

This overview explores several ways to interpret the share of unemployment. The first is where the share of unemployment can be calculated for those who are "neither employed nor in education or training" (the NEET rate), which includes non-active people.

**Youth employment break down**

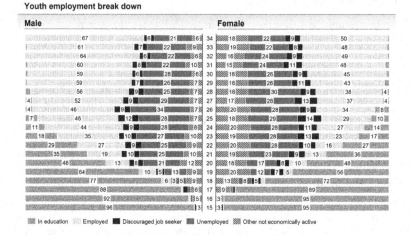

*Figure 4.4* Youth employment by gender and age.

The second excludes the non-active category, giving a more accurate perspective of unemployment ("unemployment rate"), as those who cannot work for health or family reasons. In any case, the fact that a significant proportion of the youth aged 17 and below are in education (>88 percent) or are supposed to attend school, means these age groups are excluded in the unemployment calculation.

The NEET rate for those aged between 18 and 34 is 66 percent. In most international statistics, youth unemployment refers to the age range of 18–24-year-olds. The NEET rate for this age range in South Africa is 82 percent and for the age group 25–34, it is 60 percent. The unemployment rate is in any case lower than the NEET rate, which is logically the case as the unemployment rate does not incorporate the non-active category of people. The overall youth unemployment rate is 59 percent, which is 75 percent for the 18–24 cohort, and 53 percent for the 25–34 cohort (Figure 4.5).

The younger age group (18–24) is also worse off than the older youth group (25–34). The difference in the unemployment rate between the age groups is 22 percentage points or 37 percent.

In conclusion, the research shows the overall youth unemployment rate was 59 percent, and the unemployment rate for those between 18 and 24 years was 75 percent.

**Youth NEET and unemployment break down, 2021 Q2**

In %

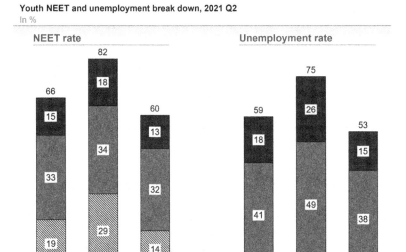

*Figure 4.5* Youth NEET and unemployment rates by age.

Going forward, this chapter will refer to unemployment in South Africa as 59 percent, reflected in the overall unemployment in the age group 18–34. The 59-percent split is 18 percent discouraged job seekers and 41 percent unemployed, leaving 41 percent employed.

These unemployment figures differ significantly from the figures often referred to by official sources and the media. The reason for the difference originates from the reference group. Internationally, the unemployment figures are typically reported as unemployed people divided by those who want to work, including those that are working, job seeking, and discouraged, but not those who are not economically active, meaning learners, parents working in the household, or sick people. The reference group used in official reports and the media in South Africa is typically the full group of people in the reference age, including leaners, parents, and sick. Consequently, the number of unemployed youth, compared to all youth, is much lower than the unemployed who want to work.

**South African youth unemployment rate over time**
In %

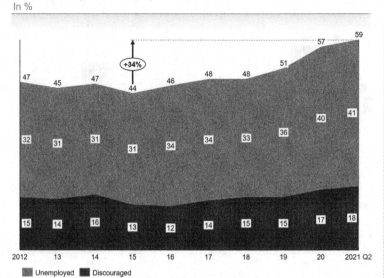

*Figure 4.6* Youth unemployment 2012–2021.

## Employment rates: The long view

Historically, the unemployment rate fluctuated between 44 percent and 48 percent between 2012 and 2018, according to StatsSA (Figure 4.6). In 2019, the rate climbed to 51 percent, pre-COVID-19. In 2020 and 2021, the pandemic and resulting lockdowns caused the rate to climb to 57 percent and 59 percent, respectively. The level of discouragement has also increased, but less sharply than the rate of those who seek employment.

## The geography

Where are the unemployed situated geographically? The segment below differentiates between urban and rural areas across the country's nine provinces: Eastern Cape, Free State, Gauteng, KwaZulu-Natal (KZN), Limpopo, Mpumalanga, Northern Cape, North West, and Western Cape (Figure 4.7).

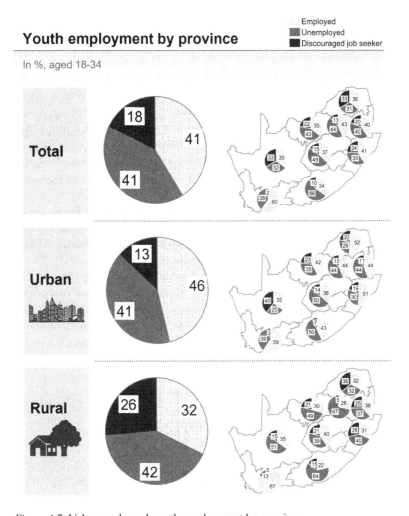

*Figure 4.7* Urban and rural youth employment by province.

In urban areas, the employment level is 46 percent, which is 5 percentage points above the national average, and 14 percentage points above rural areas. The big difference, however, is shown in the rate of discouragement between urban and rural areas. In rural areas, double the number of young people is discouraged than those in urban areas, where the rate is 13 percent.

At a provincial level, the picture is similar. Urban areas mostly have a higher employment rate than rural areas. However, there is a large disparity among provinces. While the Western Cape has an employment rate of 60 percent of the province's youth population, in the Eastern Cape it is the lowest at just 34 percent.

In urban areas, the level of discouragement is typically much lower than in rural areas, ranging from 2 percent in the Western Cape's urban areas to 40 percent in the Northern Cape. In rural areas, however, the spread is larger, ranging from as low as 5 percent in the Western Cape, to 36 percent in Limpopo. Only the Northern Cape and the North West are exceptions. In these provinces, the level of discouragement is higher in urban areas than in rural areas, but this could be a result of the small sample size.

In summary, youth in urban areas are much more likely to be employed than they are in rural areas while youth living in rural areas in the Eastern Cape are statistically in the worst position in South Africa, with nearly 80 percent unemployed or discouraged.

The level of discouragement is also high in Limpopo and in the Northern Cape, where a third of the youth have given up searching for a job even though they want to work. The Western Cape, conversely, has high employment, and a low level of discouraged people in both urban and rural areas.

## Ethnic differences

The South African population, culturally and legally, differentiates between ethnicities. Typically, the classifications are black, coloured, Indian, Asian (occasionally combined as Indian/Asian), and white (Figure 4.8).

Still today, long after the official end of apartheid, there is legal discrimination along ethnic lines. Legislation was introduced by the ruling party to redress apartheid's legacy of racial inequality. Broad-based black economic empowerment is a government policy to advance economic transformation and economically empower the country's previously disadvantaged groups (blacks, Indians, and coloureds that are South African citizens). It introduces racial quotas into hiring practices, government procurement, and other areas of the economy.

The 2021 Q2 statistics reveal a significant gap between ethnicities that persists today, which is also reflected in employment figures. While only 38 percent of black youths have a job, 85 percent of white youths

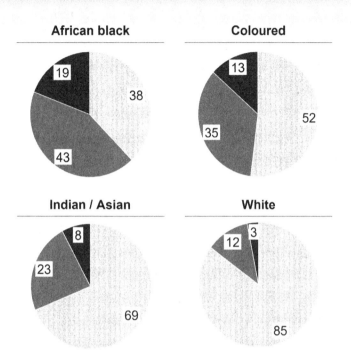

*Figure 4.8* Youth employment by ethnicity.

are employed. In-between these are coloureds at 52 percent and Indians at 69 percent. In addition, the level of discouragement is nearly seven times higher for blacks than it is for whites.

Black Africans have the worst starting point regarding employment. Only 38 percent of the youth have a job and the level of discouragement is very high at one-fifth, while four out of ten black youths are searching for a job.

One in three coloured youths are looking for a job, while every eighth coloured youth has given up looking for one. Seven out of ten Indian/ Asians have a job. Nearly nine out of ten young whites have a job, while the level of discouragement is very low, at 3 percent.

## Impact of qualifications

Qualification levels have an impact on the chance of a youth being employed or unemployed. The following illustration shows which share of unemployed and discouraged youth per their educational attainment. Out of the 59 percent unemployed and discouraged youth, 5 percent have primary education or less, 44 percent have not completed secondary education while 42 percent have done so, and 9 percent have a tertiary education (Figure 4.9).

These statistics also highlight the fact that educational levels among young unemployed South Africans are very low. About half do not have a secondary school qualification.

The chart below (Figure 4.10), Youth Employment by Group, examines the employment rates based on the educational levels identified above.

In the group of primary and lower education as well as in the category of those who have not completed secondary school, more than 60 percent of youth are unemployed or discouraged. The percentage of employment increases by 6 percentage points for the youth that have completed secondary school. The employment rate of tertiary graduates, including universities (youth with degrees) or vocational

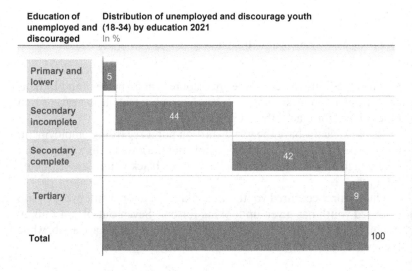

*Figure 4.9* Youth unemployment by qualification.

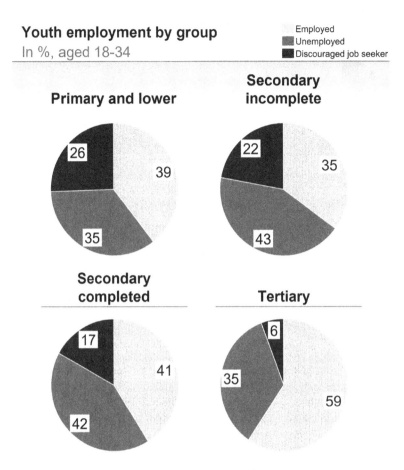

*Figure 4.10* Youth employment by education levels.

institutions (youth with diplomas), is at nearly 60 percent, with a low discouragement rate of only 6 percent.

These statistics show that the longer youth attend school, the higher their likelihood of their being employed, and the lower their level of desperation.

## Types of employment

The chart below, Youth Employment by Type, illustrates the share of formal and informal employment and the level of entrepreneurship among the youth.

**Employment by type**
In %, aged 18-34

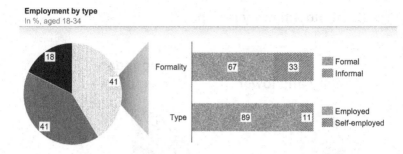

*Figure 4.11* Youth employment by type.

StatsSA defines informal employment as follows:

> This indicator is intended to identify persons who are in precarious employment situations. It includes all persons in the informal sector. Employees in the formal sector and persons employed in private households who are NOT entitled to basic benefits such as pensions or medical aid and who do not have a written contract of employment.

Of the 41 percent youth who are employed, 33 percent have an informal job. Consequently, only 27 percent of all youth in the labour force have a formal job, while 14 percent have an informal job (Figure 4.11).

Eleven percent of those that are employed are self-employed, while 89 percent work for someone else.

## Bibliography

Gapminder (2021). *Gapminder tools*. [online].

IRR (2016). *South African survey 2017*. Johannesburg: South African Institute of Race Relations.

SA Government (2016). *Electoral Commission on 2016 municipal elections.*

Statistics South Africa (2008). Concepts and definitions used in the Quarterly Labour Force Survey: Report number: 02-11-01.

Statistics South Africa (2015). National and provincial labour market: Youth: Q1: 2008-Q1: 2015.

Statistics South Africa (2021). Quarterly Labour Force Survey: (2nd Quarter 2021).

Van Broekhuizen, H., & van der Berg, S. (2013). *How high is graduate unemployment in South Africa?: A much-needed update.* Econ3x3.

World DataBank (2015). *World development indicators.* World DataBank
World DataBank (2021a). *GDP per capita (current US$) – South Africa.* World
    DataBank
World DataBank (2021b). *Gini index (World Bank estimate).* World DataBank
World Population Review (2021). *Gini coefficient by country 2021.* World
    Population Review [online].
Expert interviews
Participating observations

# 5    The 11 drivers of youth employment

Let us take one step back at this point in the book. So far you have got an impression of how unemployed youth live in South Africa, what challenges they face, and what drives them. You have also got some context around the figures quantifying youth unemployment in the country. Hopefully by now you have a decent understanding of the situation with regard to this topic in South Africa.

This book aims to build scenarios to describe possible future states of youth unemployment in 2040. To approach these scenarios, we now need to understand which elements drive future employment and how they can develop over the timeframe of the scenarios.

This chapter combines the insights from the field, those from the experts, and the statistical data to describe the 11 drivers of youth employment. These drivers are independent of South Africa's specific circumstances, but each of them has sub-drivers that take account of the local context. Therefore, this chapter lays the foundation for the scenarios while also highlighting the factors that need to be in place to change the trajectory of youth unemployment.

The 11 drivers are split into labour demand, labour supply, and employment enablers, as illustrated in Figure 5.1.

### Driver 1: Number of available jobs

As a driver of employment, the number of available jobs is highly relevant, but it will not necessarily solve the problem as the available jobs can require higher qualifications and more experience than young people have, and they could be far from where people live. Secondly, job availability is understood to be linked to economic growth as a driver. However, this growth will only support employment at scale if it is in labour-intensive industries. Thirdly, further to this, particularly low-skilled jobs are likely to be automated, particularly as the world moves

DOI: 10.4324/9781003186052-6

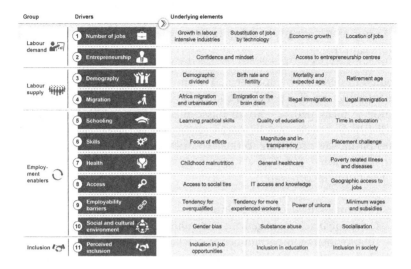

*Figure 5.1* Eleven drivers for youth employment.

towards 2040. Fourthly, the location of available jobs needs to be geographically proximate to the potential workforce.

### Economic growth and stability

At the time the main research was done for this book, the South African economy was nearly at a standstill, with GDP growth of only 1.4 percent in 2017, 0.8 percent in 2018 as the economy slid into recession, and just 0.2 percent in 2019. The economy, already in a precarious situation when COVID-19 hit the country and pandemic-related lockdowns led to negative growth of nearly minus 7 percent in 2020 compared to the previous year.

In 2017, two global ratings agencies – Fitch and Standard & Poor's – downgraded South Africa's full credit rating to sub-investment grade or junk status, citing the dominance of politics in policy making, a weak economy, and a deterioration in public finances, among other factors. The downgrades came in the wake of questionable economic policy decisions and cabinet reshuffles by former president Jacob Zuma. The downgrades affected foreign investment, weakened the Rand, and made borrowing more expensive.

These factors had an impact on the reputation of South Africa as an investment destination and affected trust in Zuma's administration, particularly following a slew of leaked emails showing that he had, through a network of personal contacts, undermined state institutions in favour of his friends and family in a process that became known as "state capture".

South Africa has implemented certain laws to overcome the structural inequalities created by apartheid. The most radical and contentious is the introduction of a policy to address apartheid's economic marginalisation of black people – Broad-Based Black Economic Empowerment or B-BBEE. It sets racially based requirements for employment and rates businesses according to their contribution to B-BBEE and racial transformation.

The rating incorporates:

- Percentage of black ownership.
- Levels of black management and control.
- Employment equity (number of black employees).
- Skills development of previously disadvantaged groups.
- Preferential procurement for companies considered to be previously disadvantaged.
- Enterprise development.
- Socioeconomic development.
- Qualifying of small enterprises.

A high rating increases a company's chance of winning government tenders. As the rating is carried through the supply chain, those affected include companies that do not directly apply for government tenders but are linked to companies that do. B-BBEE opened the door for upward mobility, but its impact has not been optimal. It has created an extremely wealthy group of companies and individuals at one end of the spectrum and although it has had an impact on the overall growth of employment and empowerment of people lower down the chain, the process remains one largely of redistribution of existing wealth through share schemes and job reservation rather than the growth of new companies that in turn create new jobs.

Government jobs are often given to friends and family members of well-placed politicians while government-linked contracts are also frequently linked to patronage, referred to by the ruling party as "cadre deployment," rather than merit. State-owned companies tend to be run by party loyalists. This skews the job market and reduces the number of available formal jobs for people without those networks.

This practice became more prominent under Zuma. His networks were positioned in places where they were able to steal billions of rands through crooked contracts and other corrupt practices. According to *The Economist* magazine, "Mr Zuma hollowed out institutions, appointed crooks and liars to senior jobs and ensured that the watchdogs who are supposed to stop corruption were muzzled." The magazine claims that without state capture led by Zuma, the South African economy could be 25 percent larger than it is.

When the head of the ruling African National Congress (ANC) party, Cyril Ramaphosa, took over as president following the ousting of Zuma by the party in 2018, expectations of change were high. He had a reputation for being a competent politician with great integrity who had made his own personal fortune through his business pursuits rather than from politics. Ramaphosa promised to investigate state capture and bring the offenders to book but the process has been slow and had little result. This is despite a slew of dramatic disclosures about the extent of state capture by an array of politicians, businesspeople, and others before the Zondo Commission, a public inquiry set up by, ironically, Zuma, in January 2018 to investigate allegations of state capture, corruption, fraud, and other issues in government and the public sector.

Ramaphosa has had to manage the resurgence of demands by sections of his party and others for the expropriation of land in South Africa without compensation. This conversation is popular among disadvantaged voter groups but has met fierce resistance from business, international investors, and property owners. It is generally held that such an initiative could further weaken international trust in South Africa's economy, with critics pointing to the near collapse of the economy of neighbouring Zimbabwe in the wake of widespread land seizures there.

A major problem South Africa faces, particularly given low growth and high unemployment, is the huge inequality gap – one of the biggest globally. Just 10 percent of income earners account for 66 percent of the income. This figure has risen from 57 percent at the end of apartheid in 1993. The income growth of the top one percent of earners has increased by 50 percent in the same period. On the other side of the spectrum, the poorest half of South Africans have lost 30 percent of their income since the ANC took power in 1994.

The gap is partly addressed by monthly grants, but this has been criticised as unsustainable, given the numbers. In 2019/2020, more than 18 million grant recipients were funded by about five million taxpayers, with the latter number declining because of growing emigration. In 1996/1997, the number South Africans who relied on government grants was just three million.

## Growth in labour-intensive industries

Economic growth supports employment, but only if the growth results in newly created jobs. In South Africa, the national employment rate in labour intensive industries such as agriculture, mining, and manufacturing dropped from 30 percent in 2000 to 19 percent today, mostly driven by industrialisation and a shift of the economy towards service-related industries. More than 72 percent, of employment is now in service-related industries, which typically require higher skill sets and are therefore inaccessible to under-educated youth.

Not only has the employment in labour intensive industries decreased, but the number of jobs overall has decreased. There were about 170,000 fewer available jobs in 2016 than there were in 2008, equating to a loss of 60 jobs each day. During the same time period, the number of young people grew by 1,260,000, equating to 380 new-borns per day. This discrepancy shows the already severe challenge face the country on the unemployment front.

## Impact of Industry 4.0

The already precarious employment situation in South Africa faces another challenge – the growth of technology-based jobs and services and automation, or the so-called fourth industrial revolution (4IR). This is already resulting in the substitution of humans with automated systems and artificial intelligence, and even robots, which can undertake repetitive physical work. McKinsey & Company, a consulting firm, claims that artificial intelligence will contribute to economic growth three to four times more by 2030 than it does today. This will widen the divide between countries prepared for 4IR's technological disruption of the workplace – advanced economies in Europe, the Americas, and parts of Asia – and the rest and also between urban and rural areas within underdeveloped countries.

Even though job substitution might be more prevalent in highly developed countries, 41 percent of all work activities in South Africa have the potential to be automated, including those in office administration, banks, factories, the travel industry, and logistics.

The ongoing substitution of work will create jobs that do not exist today, widening skills shortages and dramatically increasing the need for skills development. The world is in a situation where 65 percent of children globally who are entering primary education today will work in jobs that have yet to be invented.

This transition from traditional work to future jobs and from labour to capital has major implications for companies and society at large.

Companies have to change their recruitment processes and seek new skills in the increasingly competitive talent market. Universities, too, will be affected as they try to keep up with changing needs. Remote working resulting from the COVID-19 pandemic has already started a shift in this direction.

Reskilling is a significant cost for companies looking at more tech-driven business models and it is not practical for companies to do so unless it makes commercial sense. The jobs of the future will require not just technical expertise but also soft skills, such as interpersonal skills, judgement, and complexity management.

It is likely that the workforce will become younger, attracting tech-savvy people while those in more traditional jobs may be less open to change. These trends will lead to new business models and work environments that may not always be employment friendly. In such a transition, job losses are inevitable.

South Africa has a complicating factor – the country's powerful trade unions who appear more inclined to push for revenue benefits for workers already in jobs than to engage on other serious problems facing employment in the country, including inevitable changes in the workplace.

Monga and McGaughey, public policy and economics researchers, argue on the contrary that, throughout world history, technological advancements and the introduction of new machines have only replaced human labour in the short term but created many more jobs than they destroyed in the long term. As the adage goes, "humans will find other things to do."

The transition to the new jobs of the future is an opportunity for the youth of South Africa, but only for those with education and they are already the main beneficiaries already of employment. Interventions in the education system are urgent to start changing the situation at this level for future needs.

The question arises as how to create employment in an environment of declining job growth. Discussion about the viability of introducing a universal basic income (UBI) system has gained traction in the wake of COVID-19 to enable people to survive and to generate economic activity, albeit at a low level. The question is whether South Africa can afford it, given the combination of low growth, high and growing debt, and mediocre political leadership and policy.

## Impact of a UBI

UBI is an equal payment going to every citizen of a country, regardless of their age, socioeconomic status, wealth, or employment status. The driving idea behind a UBI is to reduce bureaucracy for individualised grants, reduce social stigma attached to grants, and most importantly, provide a solution for potential mass unemployment as jobs get presumably substituted by technology. Additionally, economic opportunities are redistributed. Considering the low savings rate of small income earners, a UBI should stimulate economic activities.

The idea dates back to the late 1700s, introduced by philosopher and political theorist Thomas Paine, a founding father of the United States of America. Even Milton Friedman, a Nobel prize laureate for economics, picked up the idea, seeing it as a way to correct inequalities created by the free market.

Critics state that a UBI does not replace the value of human work but rather disincentivises people from finding work. There have been several trials for a UBI, for example in Canada, Kenya, Brazil, and Finland, and even Namibia.

But success has been elusive. The trials were either not set up properly, they have not been academically sound, lacked a control group, or have not published results yet. It therefore is not clear whether a UBI will work in practice.

Universal fair incomes, also typically government funded, are another support mechanism. In contrast to the UBI, these are intended to provide social security just for those in need, such as children, the sick, or retired people.

South Africa has, in the wake of COVID-19, considered the viability of introducing a state-funded basic income grant. The idea is not new. The main opposition Democratic Alliance party demanded such an intervention back in 2002 and by 2020, the country already had 31 percent of its population relying on social grants – 18.29 million out of a population of 59.6 million.

A UBI would be fair and would help break up ossified inequalities like the gender wage gap and ethnic and social economic differences. However, as noted above, trials to date have not been conclusive, with the results not being clear or not academically rigorous. First indications are not necessarily positive. The Namibian government has claimed that its people had become lazy on the back of it.

South Africa's social grants system has already been criticised for disincentivising people from becoming economically active. It has also not proven to be very effective.

A special unemployment grant – the Social Relief of Distress (SRD) grant – of R350 for each qualifying person to address COVID-19-induced hardships was launched in May 2020, called the SRD. It was intended to assist about nine million people who encountered economic hardship as a result of lockdowns, but it fell victim to corruption and maladministration. Only 600,000 people out of about 15 million South Africans the grant was intended for were paid out, while 60 percent of eligible applicants were falsely rejected.

In late 2021, the government was considering options as the SRD grant was set to expire in early 2022. One of the options on the table was a basic income grant. Others included an extension of the presidential employment stimulus programme, a job seeker allowance, and a family grants as implemented in Brazil.

## *The geography of employment*

Segregation of ethnicities was the underlying principle of apartheid. One of the techniques to enforce segregation was the relocation of people of colour. Townships were built far from city centres, having geometrical layouts, with controllable entry and exit points, and zoning according to ethnicity, and even language. It also drove the creation of so-called homelands, where areas of "self rule" for the black majority were established in parts of the country, some of them far from jobs and urban areas.

The post-apartheid government paradoxically reinforced spatial inequality. Instead of building high-rise buildings in proximity to commercial centres, informal settlements were converted to formal settlements. Government-financed houses with title deeds were given to the previously disadvantaged but many of these were located in remote townships, or in the former rural homelands, where there were neither jobs, nor effective public transport systems.

The South African public transport system is notoriously under-developed and poorly run. The rail and tram systems functioning during apartheid either stopped operating or became unreliable. There have been efforts to reboot the public transport system. In Johannesburg, the Metrobus system was started in the 2000s, and in 2009 the competitive Rea Vaya bus system was introduced, with a view to boosting transport for the 2010 Soccer World Cup.

In 2012, the pricey high-speed Gautrain was introduced for white collar commuters within and between Johannesburg and Pretoria as well as to OR Tambo International Airport. Tuk-tuks and ride hailing services, like Uber, were added to the mix, but they also attract middle to higher income passengers.

The backbone of the transportation system is the privately run taxi industry using minibuses and minivans. They typically pick up passengers along the street, if stopped by a hand sign indicating the destination, or at taxi ranks. They commute within townships and connect townships to business districts and also run long distance between cities. They are used mainly by the poorer population as they are the cheapest means of transport.

Many people also used to use government suburban trains, but most are defunct today due to vandalism and a lack of investment and maintenance. The success of the costly Rea Vaya bus system has been patchy, but mostly it remains dysfunctional.

Due to the remoteness of the low income residential and the commercial areas, workers and prospective workers are dependent on taxi transport. A suburban, mainly white employee's commute is 88 minutes a day. For a disadvantaged worker in the townships, this commute can easily add up to four hours every day.

Although the fares seem low for a single ride (±R5–R25 depending on distance and provider), they add up and are the largest expense for low-income workers, with the costs exceeding that of accommodation or food.

While transport costs amount to an average of R560 a month for jobseekers, job-seeking youth only have on average around R527 available in a month. As a result, many young people give up looking for a job simply because they cannot afford to pay for the transport.

Economic growth only drives employment if the jobs and labour are geographically proximate or overlapping. Most jobs in South Africa are in the large urban areas and metros of Johannesburg, Pretoria, Cape Town, Durban, and Gqeberha (called Port Elizabeth until a name change in 2021).

In urban areas, the highest density residential areas are inner cities and townships, which are also home to the most disadvantaged populations. The available (formal) jobs, however, are typically in business areas such as Sandton or the Cape Town central business district, or in industrial areas that are further away from townships, with limited accessibility, such as Kempton Park in Gauteng. This is a legacy of apartheid spatial design and planning, which intended to limit black urbanisation. This remains a challenge and one that has not sufficiently been addressed since the end of apartheid in 1994.

However, the areas with the highest youth unemployment are rural areas, as outlined in Chapter 4. An example is Bushbuckridge, a large rural area remote from any major city, where the youth unemployment rate of about 75 percent, is among the highest in the country as barely any job opportunities exist. The jobs are simply not located near to where the unemployed youth are who so desperately need them.

## Driver 2: Building entrepreneurship

Formal employment is not the only route to a job. Many Africans across the continent have started their own businesses in order to survive. Many fail but some do grow to become mid-sized companies or larger. Sometimes people start small trading businesses or become self-employed, delivering services and products to bigger companies.

However, in South Africa, the self-employment or start-up rate among the youth is low. The question is why more young people not starting their own businesses. They have ideas, but their hard and soft skills may not be sufficiently developed to take those ideas forward. It is also worth noting that townships have huge purchasing power and market gaps, which makes them a potential breeding ground for entrepreneurs.

The World Bank estimates that in 2014, the township of Diepsloot, one of the medium-sized and notoriously dangerous Johannesburg townships, had a GDP of R671 million. Many foreign traders move into these gaps, causing resentment among township residents.

### *Confidence and mindset*

Several young unemployed South Africans have business ideas, even if they are small. A girl in East London wanted to start a muffin bakery and sell her products in her township neighbourhood. She did not know where to start and was pre-occupied with financial concerns. A lack of confidence, though, was the biggest constraint to her realising her dream.

A study on entrepreneurial activities in South Africa investigated start-ups in the Western Cape to understand the impact of hard skills on the one hand and soft skills on the other. Those start-ups that were trained in hard skills or formal business administration such as accounting, management, and human resources performed worse than start-ups without any training. The highest performance was achieved by those given psychological training, such as goal setting, feedback mechanisms, and managing setbacks. Even short confidence-building courses such as bootcamps can help young people to succeed in business.

The path to success is clearly to build confidence in young people to enable them to step outside their comfort zones and be brave enough to embark on a journey that may be successful but could also end in failure; to plant the seed of self-employment as a means of generating income.

### *Access to entrepreneurship centres*

Besides starting new enterprises, growing them from the first to the second and third employee is crucial. Structured support is required.

South Africa has numerous entrepreneurship support institutions and incubators. The Aspen Network lists 340 providers for entrepreneurship support in South Africa.

There are numerous national and provincial government agencies and programmes, such as the extended public works programme, the National Empowerment Fund, the Eskom Economic Empowerment Programmes and those established by provincial government agencies, such as the Gauteng Enterprise Propeller, the municipal govern-ment agency JoziHub, and a range of private sector programmes and incubators. Training is also offered by educational institutes such as business schools, and nine entrepreneurship skills training programmes, such as the Branson Centre for Entrepreneurship.

However, most of these institutions and programmes do not target unemployed and under-qualified youth. Still, in helping to grow small businesses, there will be an incremental increase in jobs.

## Driver 3: Demographic shifts

According to the simplest labour market perspective, there is supply and demand for labour, supply being the workers and demand being the jobs. To achieve higher employment rates, there must to be more jobs or fewer people wanting to work.

To understand the dynamics of workforce availability, South Africa's population shifts in terms of birth and fertility rates, mortality rates, life expectancy, and retirement age are examined with a view to understanding whether or not South Africa is enjoying a demographic dividend or is likely to do so in the future.

### *Birth rate and fertility*

The fertility rate in South Africa is 2.34 (the latest figure as of 2015), meaning each woman, on average, has 2.34 children. This rate has dropped significantly from 3.66 in 1990. This typically indicates an improved level of social security that often comes hand-in-hand with urbanisation and a growing middle class. The higher the likelihood of children dying is, or the weaker the support system for the elderly, the more children are born to provide security for the family.

Other countries with similar per capita GDP rate, however, have lower fertility rates. Brazil is at 2.07 and Thailand at 1.54. Child mor-tality in South Africa is at 75 deaths per 1,000 births. This figure is higher than comparable countries like Brazil, at 23, and Thailand at 18.

*Life expectancy*

The life expectancy in South Africa is 62.4 years. Countries with a similar per capita GDP have a higher life expectancy. In Brazil it is 72, in Thailand 73, and Costa Rica 79. In fact, hardly any developing country has a lower life expectancy, except perhaps Afghanistan. Reasons for this are outlined in the health chapter. However, the life expectancy has improved, rising from about 40 years in the 1940s to 64 years in 1994, when the apartheid era officially ended. In just over 10 years from 1994, up to 2006, life expectancy plummeted by more than 10 years to 51 – similar to that of South Africa in the 1950s.

The main reason for this development was the AIDS denialism that was a feature of former president Thabo Mbeki's rule from 1999 to 2008, during which time the government denied HIV-positive people access to antiretrovirals. Since he left power and the policy changed to include the roll out of antiretrovirals, life expectancy increased to today's 62.4 years.

The child mortality rate of 7.5 percent means that of the 2.34 children per woman, 2.16 survive. As women on average become pregnant early, even in their teens, combined with an increasing life expectancy, the resulting population growth rate is typically much higher than the economic growth rate.

In South Africa, the retirement age is between 60 and 65 years. Citizens or permanent residents and refugees can receive the "older person's grant" from the age of 60 if they do not have any other means of financial income. The grant covers a monthly payment of R1,890 until the age of 75. Thereafter, R1,910 will be paid.

*Demographic dividend*

The demographic dividend is a "window period for economic growth created when a country's fertility rates decline and the working-age population grows." To address this window of opportunity, it is necessary that: the working age population increases relative to the overall population; policies allow for accompanying economic growth; and the transitions happen quickly. Ultimately, however, without the economic participation of the working age population, there is no demographic dividend. This is the case in South Africa, as things stand.

The working age population, categorised as being those from 16 to 65 is likely to grow by 25 percent from 2015 to 2040 in absolute terms, and by 3.5 percent in relative terms (Figure 5.2).

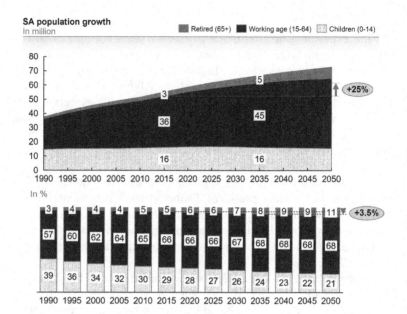

*Figure 5.2* Demographic dividend in South Africa.

South Africa is in the state of an "advanced transition," meaning that the demographic shift, lower fertility rates, and the lower mortality rate, are in full swing. The window of a growing working age population looks set to continue until about 2045, after which the working age population will shrink due to the older generation getting to retirement age and fewer young people entering the workforce. This closes the window of opportunity.

Based on UN projections, there is a logical dependency ratio of 34 percent, meaning 34 percent of the population depends on the 66 percent of the population of working age. Continued growth of the working age population implies, theoretically, that South Africa could enjoy a demographic dividend.

However, practically speaking, a demographic dividend is only realistic if the working age population does actually work. In South Africa, half of those aged 18–34 are not working, and about a third of the older generation is not employed. The dependency ratio in rural South Africa is 78 percent and in urban areas it is 68 percent. Combined, it is 74 percent (Figure 5.3).

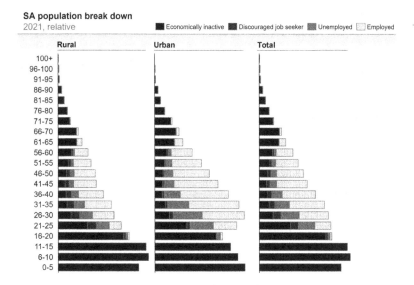

*Figure 5.3* Employment distribution in South Africa.

This huge difference of the theoretical dependency ratio of 34 percent to the actual ratio of 74 percent illustrates that there is no demographic dividend in South Africa. With the extremely high unemployment levels in South Africa, the country is not likely to harness its potential for a demographic dividend, particularly as the demographic shift is already at an advanced stage as the rate of young people entering the workforce is declining compared to the portion of the population the workforce has to carry, that is the children and elderly.

### Retirement age

In South Africa, the retirement age is most commonly between 60 and 65 years of age. Citizens or permanent residents and refugees can receive the "older person's grant" starting aged 60 if they do not have any major means of financial income. The grant covers a monthly payment of just under ZAR 2,000.

The retirement age is relevant for youth employment. The sooner experienced workers retire and the less total time they spend in the labour force, the more youth will have the opportunity to become employed. However, the incentive to retire in South Africa is not given for the large portion of the population that was not able to generate significant savings, considering the lack of a government pension with the rather limited "older person's grant."

In many Western and Northern countries where youth unemployment is not of concern, the retirement age increases to reduce the burden of the working population to carry the social system.

## Driver 4: Migration patterns

Besides demographic shifts, the supply of labour can also be determined by migration patterns. There can be an influx and an outflux of people into South Africa, which can be legal or illegal, and driven by economic or political issues.

### *Migration and urbanisation*

Thirty-two million Africans, or 13.4 percent of the African population, are migrants who live outside their home country. As many as 16.4 million of them live in other African countries. A majority 87 percent of migrants in Africa tend to move to a neighbouring country, while 8.9 million African migrants live in Europe, 4.1 million in Asia, and 1.7 million in the United States.

Urbanisation is a global trend as work opportunities, safety, quality of life, education, and upward mobility become regarded as being superior to a rural lifestyle. It drives an increase in per capita incomes. Between 2017 and 2050, Africa's urban population is projected to triple.

In South Africa, the population of Johannesburg is projected to grow by about 32 percent between 2020 and 2040 to 7.5 million inhabitants. At the same time, Cape Town will grow by about 30 percent to 4.5 million people over this period.

### *Legal and illegal immigration*

About 6 percent of people living in South Africa are foreign citizens, adding up to about 3.6 million immigrants. Of residence permits given in 2012, 41 percent were given to youth within an age range of 15–35, with 29 percent of the permits being employment related.

South Africa grants work visas to foreigners if they possess critical skills. The list contains skills that are difficult to obtain and are sometimes rare, for example astronomers, but it also mentions skills that are obtainable quickly or without formal education, for example sheep shearers or welders. The list was updated in 2021. However, at time of publication, the revised critical skills list has not been ratified.

Out of 229 critical skills needed in South Africa, most are the type acquired in a trade school or vocational college, which is known as a Technical and Vocational Education and Training (TVET) college in South Africa. The fact that foreigners are allowed to occupy these manual trades indicates that South Africa is not producing sufficient tradesmen for its needs.

South Africa is a magnet for illegal immigrants, mostly from other African countries, who seek better lives in Africa's most sophisticated economy. The largest number of illegal immigrants are from neighbouring Zimbabwe. The economically distressed country produces highly qualified workers and is said to have one of the best schooling systems in Southern Africa. But there are also large numbers of Mozambicans, Nigerians, Somalians, and Ethiopians, among others, resident in South Africa – both legally and illegally.

Illegal immigrants come with the intention of earning money to support themselves and to support their families back home. Immigrants often find jobs, such as in construction or the service industry, as they are typically preferred over South Africans due to their higher qualifications, better work ethic, and less unionisation. However, many are also attractive to employers because they are prepared accept lower wages than South Africans, which causes resentment among job seekers in their host country.

Immigrants, both legal and illegal, are known for their entrepreneurial activities. As discussed before, in Katlehong, a group of Zimbabweans selling bananas at street corner stands were able to undercut the South African sellers in price by bundling their purchasing power, and buying in bulk at lower prices.

The shrewd and proactive business activities of African foreigners and their resulting success and relative prosperity has sparked discontent among poorer South Africans. Xenophobic attacks, involving the burning down of foreign-owned businesses and chasing away their owners – and sometimes killing them – are not uncommon in townships throughout South Africa. They accuse foreigners of taking their jobs but in fact many businesses owned by foreigners employ South Africans.

### Emigration and brain drain

About 5 percent of the South African population lives outside the country. Preferred destinations include the UK, the United States, Canada, and Australia. Health professionals, including doctors and nurses, are those most sought after by other countries but increasingly skills across the board.

The biggest drivers of emigration are crime, political uncertainty, the erosion of standards and institutions, the lack of opportunities for white people in light of the strict empowerment legislation mentioned above, and a response to talent demand in other regions. The first big wave of emigration was after the end of apartheid when many white South Africans left.

Emigration of working professionals causes several challenges for an economy, particularly if those jobs are not replaced. Firstly, a country loses a part of its tax basis. Secondly, skills are lost to the country, particularly in specialist areas such as health, ICT, engineering, and others, that are hard to replace quickly. Thirdly, emigration affects confidence in the country's ability to provide a better future for successful individuals, which results in a vicious circle. All of these elements are true for South Africa. Although the country is at an early stage of emigration, the dynamics can accelerate, particularly as the pandemic restrictions are eased.

The South African government is trying to make it hard for people to emigrate, by, for example restricting the amount of money that can easily be moved out of the country and finding creative ways to prevent pensions moving abroad and finding new ways to tax emigrants.

Migration is a more uncertain factor than demographics. Political, economic, and humanitarian crises in neighbouring countries can result in massive migration, as has happened with Zimbabweans coming to South Africa. Of course, the opposite can happen too. The size of the potential workforce can therefore fluctuate, based on the stability and attractiveness of either the region or of single countries.

A relevant factor in this regard is the level of qualifications of the incoming or exiting workforce, and whether their immigration is legal or illegal. Many of those emigrating are professionals whose jobs require specific skills and experience, while immigrants with engineering and other qualifications from their home countries are working as waiters and Uber drivers due to empowerment restrictions in South Africa. These developments further squeeze unqualified South Africans out of the job market.

## Driver 5: Schooling

The quality of and access to decent education and schools in South Africa is one of the biggest factors affecting employment. It is the single most cited reason for the severe unemployment situation. The problems are current as well as historical. With its pernicious Bantu education policies, the apartheid regime ring-fenced non-whites from educational attainment and economic empowerment. The continuing apartheid spatial development design can be extended to education. The poorer schools were mostly in townships and in rural areas and run by the government.

However, it is not the only cause for contemporary unemployment. Even having a good education system, as Zimbabwe still has today, does not solve unemployment. It is a necessary but not sufficient element of the employment picture. The politically authoritarian government of Robert Mugabe and severe economic decline over the latter decade or so of his rule led to massive unemployment, with an unofficial estimate of 95 percent of young Zimbabweans being without a formal job.

### Time spent in education

School dropout rates in South Africa are high. A significant number of pupils do not attend school or complete their schooling. A case study by the Centre for Development and Enterprise investigated the school attendance of South African children in Grade Two (aged 7) and found the class was 100 percent full. Between Grade 2 and Grade 10 (where children are typically aged 16), dropout rates were almost zero. However, this changed thereafter, with a 19 percent dropout rate between Grade 10 and Grade 11 (where the typical age of pupils is 17), rising to 26 percent up to the final year, Grade 12.

Of those who finished Grade 12, only 68 percent obtained their final matric qualification, and just 77 percent of them had high enough grades to be eligible for tertiary education. Of the latter group, only 45 percent go on to actually obtain a university degree.

Out of the children that were in Grade Two in 2005, only 41 percent passed their matric exam and only 31 percent were eligible for tertiary education. Of these, just 14 percent finished tertiary education.

The dropout rate is driven in part by the cost of schooling, including the need for school uniforms and transportation. Drug abuse is another cause, given the tendency for drug dealers to target vulnerable pupils, starting with those aged 14 or 15.

Some families begin to push the financial burden of households onto their children while they are still at school, particularly if a family member is unable to work due to ill health, which requires them to find a source of income. A learner may also leave for health reasons, including teenage pregnancies.

Then there is the issue of poorly performing pupils being pressured to leave school if it seems they are unlikely to pass their final-year exams. Schools are ranked by their matric pass rates. The powerful South African Democratic Teachers Union (SADTU) is allied to the ANC through trade union federation The Congress of South African Trade Unions (COSATU). It is known for controlling schools and teachers and having significant influence in the South African Department of Basic Education.

It is also accused of being corrupt, with allegations that, for example it "buys" top positions for its members. This influence is abused to push learners that are unlikely to pass matric out of the schooling system in Grade 10 and Grade 11 to not compromise the matriculation pass rates in Grade 12. The union has also compromised learners by putting teachers' interests before those of pupils, encouraging them to go on strikes over wages despite the fact strikes cause schools to close temporarily, for example (Figure 5.4).

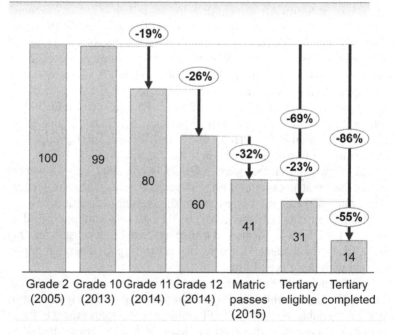

*Figure 5.4* School participation and education rates.

The high dropout rates have affected the level of qualifications in South Africa, with some people still trying to complete tertiary education at the age of 25. Nearly half of the youth in the age bracket of 25 to 34 – 43 percent – do not complete secondary school. Only one-third (34 percent) finish secondary school, and only 14 percent get tertiary education (Figure 5.5).

### Quality of education

Besides the dropout rates, the quality of the schooling system in South Africa is patchy. The country has the most unequal schooling in the world, with a significant gap between the results of the top 20 percent of students and the rest. This inequality reflects the country's overall social gap, still mostly split along ethnic lines. Consequently, only one

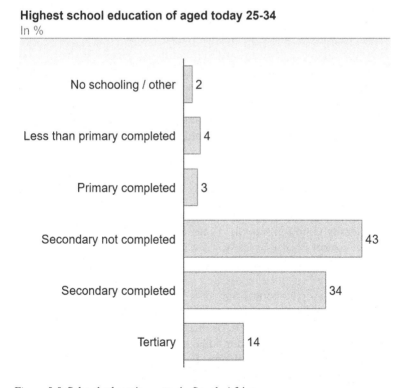

*Figure 5.5* School education rates in South Africa.

out of 200 black pupils can expect to qualify for an engineering degree, compared to one out of ten of their white counterparts.

This gap is primarily based on the double-tracked schooling system. Those who can afford it send their children to highly competitive private schools, and others to deficient public schools. The quality of teachers tends to be low in public schools, where an estimated 79 percent cannot not pass a test meant for their students. Teacher absenteeism is also high.

As a result, 14 percent of blacks and 10 percent of coloureds are illiterate, while only 3 percent of Indian and fewer than 1 percent of white South Africans are illiterate. Twelve percent of blacks and 10 percent of coloureds also experience difficulties with simple mathematical calculation. Illiteracy and innumeracy are lower among Indian/Asians and whites – about 3–4 percent – with the rate slightly higher for women than for men.

Language barriers are another challenge for children and teachers. South Africa has 11 official languages. Public schools typically teach in English or Afrikaans. However, children (aged 0–14) most often do not speak either of those languages at home. Only 9.1 percent speak Afrikaans at home, and 4.3 percent English.

For the other 86.5 percent of children, the languages in their homes are not used in most schools, while many teachers also do not do instruction in their mother tongue. The language issue also affects parents' ability to assist children with homework.

Introducing English and Afrikaans as secondary languages at home or in early school years would help to address this learning barrier.

### Learning practical skills

Despite the huge skills gap in South Africa, practical and soft skills are not generally taught in schools. Typically, internships are not required, either at school or at university. As a result, employers complain that school and university graduates lack practical skills needed in the workplace.

Even in dual (theoretical and practical) education, such as TVET or vocational colleges, the learning of practical skills is insufficient and technologies used are outdated, or unavailable.

As suggested earlier, a better education system will not, on its own, solve the unemployment problem. The biggest advantage of a good educational system is social permeability. Currently, the two-tier educational system enforces inequality. A high-quality school system in both the public and private sectors would increase the possibility of upward social mobility.

## Driver 6: Skills development

South Africa has multiple systems to document the level of a qualification. One is the National Qualifications Framework (NQF), which covers more than 16,000 qualifications, including those at school and university. Vocational training falls under three different entry qualification frameworks, namely the National Certificate (Vocational), the Nated System, and the Occupational Subframework, all of which provide different certificates and diplomas. This unduly complex system does not add value for learners, parents, and potential employers.

About 1.3 million learners were enrolled in vocational training in 2015 in South Africa. There are four types of institutions that offer undertake vocational training: 50 public TVET colleges with about 260 campuses; private providers covering about 205 private colleges; about 7,500 private skills providers; and 125–150 private higher educational institutions. There are also Sector Education and Training Authorities (SETAs), governing bodies for skills development in different sectors.

Lastly, there is Community Education and Training (CET) organised in nine public colleges, and about 2,640 learning centres, formerly known as Adult Basic Education and Training.

Despite efforts to simplify the magnitude of frameworks, institutions, and qualifications, employers, and learners can easily get lost in this complex system.

### *Intransparency*

The above shows that the problem is not a lack of available skills training offerings. The question is whether these programmes help young people to find an occupation. Dropout rates and low placement rates are the key challenge.

Only about 60 percent of students starting a TVET course will complete a diploma. The content of most programmes is not driven by the needs of employers. Most public or private TVET colleges base their course offerings on funding available from SETAs, whose performance is undermined by poor management and opaque data.

TVET colleges train for occupations, but do not necessarily train for available jobs. As a result, placement rates are low, sometimes below 10 percent, although the better programmes can achieve placement rates of up to 75 percent.

Harambee is the largest private-public-partnership employment upskilling organisation in South Africa. Harambee has so far assessed about 1.5 million disadvantaged unemployed South Africans. However, their placement rate with ~40,000 job matchings is low, at 2.6 percent.

## Lack of focus

The disconnect between employers and training institutions reflects in the lack of focus by the latter on the professions that are in demand. Employers have little input into the development of curricula so even if youth get a qualification, their skills may not be compatible with employers' needs.

More than 70 percent of education is classroom-based, and where there are not practical. Furthermore, the practical components of college tuition are often outdated. A car mechanic trained on a 1980s Mazda will be inevitably less valuable than someone trained on a modern car.

The Department of Higher Education and Training has identified the need for an employer-driven dual education. In 2019, it established the Centres of Specialisation pilot programme to address shortages in the trades and skills identified as priorities for national development and improve the public TVET college system so it is able to deliver high-quality trade qualifications that meet the needs of employers.

The aim is similar to the German model of work experience: workspace-based practical expertise combined with classroom-based theory. The centres will offer programmes that will be co-developed with employers to make the qualifications more relevant to economic needs and less theoretical than current diplomas.

## Exploiting the system

A number of incentives are provided to companies that provide the practical experience component as part of learnerships. These include funding from SETAs, B-BBEE-related tax breaks, partial re-imbursements for their costs, and Black economic empowerment (BEE) score benefits, such as preferential treatment in the awarding of tenders. This attracts them to provide such learnerships, even if they do not intend to recruit new employees from this pool of people.

But this situation can be exploited with people continuing to carry on doing one learnership after another rather than looking for a job, especially as students also receive financial support for food and transport while they are studying.

The current disconnect between employers, training institutions, and the youth has led to an opaque jungle of offerings, few of which are driven by demand from business, nor co-developed with employers. A strong model that links these three interest groups and develops a strong demand-led approach to training could revolutionise skills development in South Africa and bridge the unemployment gap.

There are many examples around the world of such models that could be implemented with the right political will. For example, in Germany, Switzerland, and Austria, the schooling system provides an alternative for those learners that do not have an aptitude for a strictly academic curriculum, and do not stay in school for the full 12 years.

This is a dual-education or apprenticeship model, which learners typically enter after Grade 9 or 10. It combines classroom learning with real life exposure, often in blocks of three months or more, switching between school and employers. Dual education includes white-collar professions, such as administration and banking, as well as blue-collar professions, such as carpentry and plumbing. The high level of practical skills offered, the exposure to the working environment, and the contact with specific employers increase placement rate for youths who have been through this system. About 80 percent of graduates in Germany find work within three months after completion, although in that country, demand for apprentices exceeds supply – a different situation to that in South Africa.

## Driver 7: Health issues

Health is an enabling factor for youth employment. Health issues can either affect the youth's ability to go to school or work directly or indirectly, for example where family members – including the breadwinner – suffer from ill health. It can lead to children dropping out of school to earn an income and take over household responsibilities, or missing classes.

### *General healthcare*

South Africa has a dual health care system, with a private, highly specialised and internationally reputed system existing alongside a free but generally low-quality public health system. Only about 16 percent of South Africans were covered by health insurance in 2018. Of these, just about 10 percent were black people.

The private sector system attracts the most spending and the most health professionals while the public system is underfinanced and poorly run, resulting in deteriorating infrastructure and low doctor-to-patient-ratios. Although South Africa's health system is expensive (8.3 percent of GDP compared to the 5 percent recommended by the World Health Organisation), health outcomes are worse than in countries with comparable income levels.

### Poverty-related illness and diseases

There are many poverty-related diseases found in South Africa, such as tuberculosis (TB), malaria, HIV/AIDS, cholera, and malnutrition. HIV prevalence for South Africans aged 15–49 is 19.1 precent, according to UNAIDS. TB is an illness with a high co-infection rate for HIV infection, and about 70 percent of TB patients are also HIV-positive. South Africa is one of the countries with the highest TB rate globally due to the comorbidity. About 10 percent of South African children, about 2 million people, are AIDS-related orphans.

HIV/AIDS is tearing families apart and burdening the youth. The disease comes with a high level of stigmatisation and low levels of social awareness. Black South Africans, in particular, do not want to be tested, as they are afraid of social exclusion. Unidentified and untreated infections lead to new infections, low quality health, and early death.

Infected and untreated parents do not only risk their children being infected, but as they lose the capacity to work, they also burden the young generation with having to take care of them, forcing youngsters to earn money and take over the family responsibilities.

### Childhood malnutrition

Childhood nutrition is a serious challenge across Africa. Malnutrition causes stunting (poor growth), marasmus (too little weight), kwashiorkor (protein deficiency), or vitamin and mineral deficiencies. These can result in attention deficit disorder, decreased IQ scores, memory deficiency, learning disabilities, reduced social skills, and reduced problem-solving abilities.

About a quarter of South African children under five years of age are stunted, 12 percent are underweight, and 5 percent wasted, all as a result of malnutrition. This all affects performance at school, which in turn will make it harder over time to compete in the job market.

Exclusive breast-feeding in the first six months prevents malnutrition in early age, but only about 25 percent of South African babies receive this. In contrast, 55 percent of the population over 15 are obese, with a rising trajectory, which is a catalyst for other health issues.

Improving health education for children and adults lowers the risk of illness and death. Making the transition to the middle class will enable more South Africans to benefit from health insurance, and to gain access to the private health system. South Africa has plans to implement a national health insurance. It remains to be seen if this leads to improved healthcare for more people or affects the quality of private healthcare even as it reduces the gap between the two.

## Driver 8: Fair access to job opportunities

In an environment with a high number of vacant jobs and available skilled people, there should be no unemployment. But access to those jobs, where they exist, is a challenge for disadvantaged South Africans. Issues include geographic proximity to areas where the jobs exist, access to IT infrastructure to search and apply for jobs, and access to social ties.

### *IT access and knowledge*

Besides geographical access to job opportunities, access to online information is a limiting factor. The lack of access to the internet and knowledge of how to use it limits access to job advertisements, information about training and upskilling and job-birding, among much else.

Nearly half – 43 percent – of young people aged 15–24 live in households without IT access, and consequently lack the knowledge of how to use the internet. Informal settlements and shacks in townships often do not have electricity and therefore cannot charge electronic devices.

Airtime and data are expensive. South Africa has the highest data cost for a large African economy. The cost for 1GB of mobile data averages at US$7.6 in South Africa. In Egypt, the same amount of mobile data costs US$1.2 (16 percent of the cost of South Africa's), US$3.1 in Nigeria (40 percent), or US$4.9 in Kenya (64 percent).

As a result, only 28 percent of youth search for jobs on the internet, according to StatsSA.

### *Access to social networks*

Jobs can be found through a transparent advertising and application process, but it also common for people to find work through their social networks. So-called "clan-based thinking" is common in South Africa. Family, friends, political affiliates, and people of the same origin or ethnic background often get preferential treatment from their own groups in the contest for jobs beyond the B-BBEE legislative push to give jobs to previously disadvantaged South Africans.

Social ties are not available to all job-searching youth. The fieldwork showed two groups of youth, namely those who grew up in an economically active area, and those who grew up in the rural areas and moved to an urban area to seek work, for example, from a village in the Eastern Cape to a Johannesburg township.

The first group is typically better connected, as they have family and friends that can help with the job search. The second group does not have this social network and struggles more to find a job. The situation is compounded by political nepotism. The example of a new fire station opening in Thokoza township, as mentioned earlier, is an example of the power of political networks in the job search process. The new jobs that opened up at the fire station were not given to the unemployed people in the community but allegedly to the friends and political cronies of the ward councillor who belonged to the ruling ANC.

### *Corruption and distance*

Many unemployed youth report that they need money to gain access to job opportunities. Paying for transport to get to job interviews is just one of the reasons they need money; the other is for bribes, which are often required for jobs in a factory, for example, where there are literally gatekeepers demanding money to give job seekers access to the right people.

Bribes may be solicited at several stages of the application process. When showing the job documents at the gate, the guard or receptionist will typically ask for a handling fee or cold drink, which is code for a bribe. The expectation is often that bank notes be inserted into the pages of the CV to enable the job seekers to even get to the next stage of the process or to the right person. Requests that the bribe be taken off the first month's salary should they get the job have not been successful.

The amount is not just a few rand; it could be as much as R500. Many do not have the money and it becomes expensive if unemployed youngsters are applying for more than one job at a time.

Geographic access, digital access, and social ties, or the lack thereof, are a legacy of the oppressive past of South Africa. In order to democratise the access to job opportunities, housing projects need to be located in the proximity of economic activities, transport needs to be cheaper and more reliable, the cost for data reduced, and the job allocation along nepotistic lines replaced by transparent, merit-based job allocations.

## Driver 9: Employability barriers

Employers looking for staff tend to prefer an older, more experienced worker to a young unemployed person. Minimum wages and the power of unions, who make it hard for under-performing staff to be fired, deter employers from hiring new entrants into the job market, especially those who lack skills and experience.

### *Minimum wages and subsidies*

Minimum wages are a hindrance to employment, increasing the jobs crisis by making it harder for new entrants to the job market.

The monthly minimum wage in South Africa, introduced in November 2016, is R20 an hour or R3,500 based on a 40-hour working week (about €230). It has led to improved wages for most low skilled workers. There are exceptions for some professions, such as farmworkers, domestic helpers, and learnerships.

But it has also made it harder for new entrants to the job market, who may be prepared to work for less than the minimum wage simply to have a job.

Another intervention in this regard was the 2014 the youth wage subsidy introduced by the Employment Tax Incentive Act. This initiative aimed to create jobs for young South Africans. Employers receive R1,000 per month for every young person under 30 that they hire. However, rather than creating new jobs, existing positions were given to younger people in the relevant age bracket, so it essentially became a jobs subsidy.

### *Power of trade unions*

Many business people believe trade unions are the single biggest barrier to employment in South Africa. Unions in South Africa have a powerful standing due to a high number of unionised workers and the affiliation of the main trade union federation, the Congress of South African Trade Unions or COSATU, to the ruling ANC along with the Communist Party of South Africa. COSATU is an amalgamation of 21 trade unions, include the teachers' union SADTU, mentioned earlier.

About 30 percent of employed South Africans are unionised, while the public sector unions have increased their membership base tenfold since the early 1990s.

The unions tend to be militant, typically objecting to dismissals, performance reviews, and redeployments of their members, often resulting in strikes. Therefore, the cost of labour, when incorporating the cost of strikes and the legal inflexibility to hire and fire workers, is not competitive, particularly compared to emerging Asian, as well as also other African countries. This compounded by the fact that South Africa has the lowest productivity growth rate among emerging economies, according to the Organization for Economic Co-operation and Development (OECD).

As Monga notes, "Unions only protect those that have a job and are a member. That is a small minority in South Africa." Because of the unions' political alliance with the ANC, the voice of this unionised worker minority is louder than other interest groups.

Additionally, unions disapprove of tax incentives or wage subsidies for young workers, fearing that it will lead to older, unionised workers losing their jobs. They also tend to prefer a confrontational approach to issues, rather than seeking co-operative solutions with employers.

### *Deficit of experience and tendency for over-qualified*

A lack of work experience is a major challenge for young people. As noted above, employers typically prefer older workers with more experience, even where they may have the same formal qualification as younger work seekers.

Many youths complain that their diplomas and certificates do not carry much weight with potential employers. The qualification system is perceived to be non-transparent or untrustworthy with regards to qualifying learners sufficiently for job readiness. Employers confirm that it is challenging to assess the true value of formal qualifications. This is an indication of the poor management of skills development programmes and their lack of alignment with employer needs, as described in the skills section above.

Another issue is the tendency for employers to hire youth who are overqualified for the job they are given, reflecting a mistrust of the education system as well as the oversupply of qualified unemployed youth willing to work in any profession. This can offset the doubts many employers have about the quality of the education system and its relevance to the broader economy and the needs of business.

It is an employer's market. As one said, "I can ask my domestic helper to have a matric certificate." This practice crowds out job seekers who do not have any qualifications, including matric.

The barriers to youth employment described above need to be addressed. The incentive of youth wage subsidies is a start, but more creative thinking is required to address challenges in this regard, particularly in improving the qualifications system to give employers more trust in this pipeline.

## Driver 10: Social and cultural environment

The microenvironment, or the "neighbourhood," has a significant influence on unemployment and health, studies have shown. For the purpose of this book, it is important to understand the dynamics the environment has on South Africa's youth employment problem. The field research highlights that socialisation, substance abuse, and gender bias are dominating elements.

### *Socialisation*

The most important environments for socialisation are the family, peers, school, and the media – both traditional and newer social media channels. All of these environments are influenced by wealth and social status. Parental care in South Africa is a challenge. Not only do families grapple with health issues that draw children into parental responsibilities, many are single parent households as a result of fathers, particularly, leaving behind their responsibilities after impregnating a woman. Only one in ten children grow up in families with two parents in South Africa.

The Maharishi Institute, a free private tertiary learning institution, tests its applicants for Post-Traumatic Stress Disorder (PTSD). This can be the consequence of a traumatic event caused by an injury, death, or the threat of it. It can cause "major depression, panic disorder, generalised anxiety disorder, and substance abuse."

The applicants to the Maharishi Institute, who tend to be previously disadvantaged South Africans from low-income areas in their late teens and early twenties, show a high rate of PTSD, with an average of 60 percent of females and 30 percent of males suffering from the condition. Violence, weak family structures, and particularly sexual abuse, as well as an unsafe childhood environment, contribute to this problem in South Africa.

### *Substance abuse*

South Africa, a country that has a thriving beer and wine industry, is known for its high levels of alcohol use. On average, a South African consumes about 10 litres of pure alcohol per year. Excluding those that do not drink at all, an alcohol-consuming South African takes in 27.1

litres of pure alcohol per year, equating to nearly 60 grams per day. Only Chad, Gambia, Mali, and Namibia have a higher per capita consumption of alcohol.

The reasons include low alcohol prices that result from local production, the easy access to bars and informal drinking establishments, and the culture of brewing alcoholic beverages at home. But it is also the result of people seeking respite from the misery or hardship of their lives.

In townships and parts of the cities, it is easy to see many intoxicated young people, even in daylight hours, hassling drivers to clean their windscreens at traffic lights, strolling around collecting bottles, or drinking on street corners in groups.

A pint of beer is about US$2.20 even in restaurants in wealthier parts of Johannesburg, which is one of the lowest rates in the world, even after purchasing power adjustments. In townships, home-brewed beer, sometimes brewed in trash bins stolen from affluent neighbourhoods, is a tradition. Alcohol, therefore, is relatively cheap and easily accessible.

Intoxication often leads to domestic violence and crime. Substance abuse does not only harm families, cause violence, and distract people from finding work, it also affects cognitive and other development.

Efforts by the government to reduce consumption, including the banning of alcohol advertising, have either not been effective or not implemented. During COVID-19, it implemented several extended bans on the purchase and transport of alcohol, although the intention was mostly to cut down on hospital beds needed for victims of the pandemic being taken up by victims of trauma or traffic accidents resulting from alcohol abuse rather than addressing the bigger picture.

### Gender bias

Women in South Africa are affected more by violence than men. They also tend to be less educated than men, with 25 percent of black women being illiterate, versus 20 percent of black men. They are further disadvantaged in other aspects of society.

The rate of women marrying young – between the ages of 10 and 29 – is high, at 34 percent versus only 21 percent of men in the same age range. Girls in some homes are still socialised to become housekeepers and child bearers. This tends to work against their participation in the economy.

Social interaction and cultural habits are formed by the everyday environment. Destructive environments reinforce themselves in a vicious cycle. To break that cycle, targeted interventions need to be set in place that keep children busy at school with afternoon activities such as sports, arts, and homework supervision. Gender issues also need to be more proactively addressed from a young age at both schools and at home.

## Driver 11: Perceived inclusion

A sense of inclusion in a community, in an ecosystem or in the broader economy is pertinent to the employment issue. First, the feeling of not being part of a majority or not having access to an opportunity can cause disruption and despair. A youth thinking that he or she is not part of society might give up even trying to contribute to that society and not adhere to the formal and informal rules of society.

Secondly, a young South African feeling he or she cannot access university because of the high cost of tertiary education might not even try to participate or may be easily engaged in protest action of one sort or another. Thirdly, the perceived lack of job opportunities results in many young people not even trying to look for a job, which is the case for 13 percent of South African youths.

### Inclusion in society and politics

An inclusive society is defined as one where people feel recognised and accepted, which leads to a sense of belonging. The inclusive society and all its members follow the same values and accept its institutions. People in the society participate in social, cultural, economic, and political life. Inclusive societies grant the same rights to everyone, including minorities, to foster non-violence, security, dignity, pluralism, solidarity, non-discrimination, and equal opportunities.

However, the field research for this book has vividly shown that disadvantaged, unemployed youth in South Africa do not feel included. The phrase uttered by some interviewees, "I don't feel like a person," is the most striking example of perceived exclusion. Young people said in interviews that they had experienced violence, lacked access to food and sanitation, that they had been discriminated against for being from a different province or country, and did not have access to opportunities. These comment show that their lack of inclusion is not a perception; it is a lived reality.

Inclusion, whether perceived or real, can lead to political disruption. Burning tyres or cars to protest against service delivery or other problems is common in the low-income areas of South Africa. Even the interviewees for this project said they perceived violence to be their only way to get attention: "If the municipality does not help us [cleaning the sanitary facilities], we burn their cars or block the road," said one of the interviewed youth.

The question arises as to what drives the need to express dissatisfaction through violence, and what the underlying beliefs are of those that take this route. Experts claim that the political culture in South Africa has inculcated a high level of distrust towards governmental institutions, based on false narratives and broken promises to the electorate.

Most famously, Bell Pottinger, a British public relations agency, was hired by the ruling ANC to create a political campaign around nonfactual allegations of what they termed white monopoly capital looting the black majority. It was promoted using fake accounts paid for by the Gupta family – the main protagonists in former president Zuma's "state capture" project. The main aim was to cover up the corruption of the Zuma government by diverting public attention to other issues.

Although Bell Pottinger closed its doors after a tide of negative publicity emanating from South Africa after their manipulation became known to the general public through leaked emails, the term "white monopoly capital" is still part of public discourse, emotionally embraced by many disadvantaged South Africans and Zuma supporters.

Daron Acemoglu and James Robinson, authors of the book *Why Nations Fail*, proclaim that political inclusiveness, reflected by the existence of inclusive, non-extractive institutions that support free and fair elections, is the most relevant factor for a country's success. The United States has historically represented this inclusiveness. At the other end of the spectrum, several African countries such as South Sudan or Somalia are considered to be failed states. They have not been able to grant their citizens basic rights nor include them in political decision-making, nor build functional state institutions.

### Inclusion in education

The so-called Fallist movement, which emerged in 2016 and 2017 at leading South African universities, is an example of an uprising caused by perceived exclusion, in this case in education. The protesting university students asked for the scrapping of university tuition fees to remove exclusion from higher education on financial grounds.

The movement was characterised by aggressive protests, causing major disruptions at several universities. Protests spilled into the streets, with looting of stores and arson by students. The total damage caused by these protests across South Africa amounted to nearly R800 million (about €50 million).

These protests showed that a relatively small group of university students in SA have a voice that is disproportionate to their numbers. The following question, however, arises: Is the scrapping of university fees a legitimate opportunity cost in comparison to other possible investments that might buttress youth employment?

Only 14 percent of the children starting school complete tertiary education, which can be a university or college level qualification. The share of those entering university is therefore low. About 95 percent of the small portion of students who graduate find a job, whereas only 52 percent of youth overall become employed. Those that are advantaged enough to go to university are best placed to find a job afterwards. They make up a tiny academic elite in South Africa (Figure 5.6).

As university students are already better off than most other South African youth, should they complain about university fees? Let us compare the costs to the United States, a country where student fees have

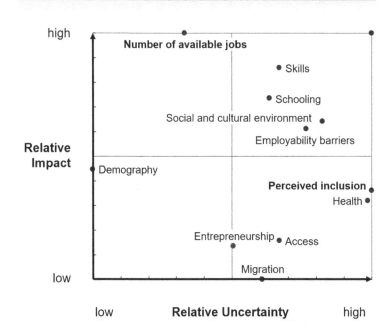

*Figure 5.6* Graduates versus non-graduates.

been widely accepted. To have a like-for-like comparison, the cost of studying an engineering degree, including tuition and accommodation, is worked out in relation to the starting salary of an engineer. The cost for a BSc. and Honour's Degree in South Africa is about twice the average starting salary (1.9 times in the country), while in the United States it is about four times that. This suggests that university fees in South Africa are about half of those in the United States.

To understand whether the universities in South Africa are particularly neglected compared to other educational institutions, compare government spending per university student to the government spending per school student. The annual spending per university student is R28,891 and R12,158 per school child. A university student thus costs the state 138 percent more than a school pupil. This shows that in fact, the South African government proportionally overspends on universities and suggests that students cannot complain about being neglected by the state, especially given the relatively high quality of tertiary education in South Africa.

### Inclusion in job opportunities

Perceived exclusion happens when the trust in being able to change the country, society, and one's own fate is severely eroded. Unemployment and giving up searching for a job are clear indicators that a society lacks inclusion. Many South Africans believe that the government is responsible for giving them a job.

Further, job seekers face issues of corruption. "We need to pay someone to even write an entry test," said one job seeker. "Police hassle us for money if we don't have a permission," said another. Access to jobs is perceived as to be non-transparent and unfair, "There are openings. But they don't really exist or are occupied already," said one interviewee.

Being excluded from job opportunities, and society in broader terms, makes young people give up hope. Fieldwork has shown that the frustration of perceived societal exclusion creates frustration, stress, and desperation.

Inclusion can be perceived as political inclusion, which includes being able to vote and have some influence over who governs, or as economic inclusion, which means having access to merit-based monetary opportunities.

South Africa has shifted from an extractive to inclusive society since the end of apartheid and is considered mostly fair, granting extensive rights to the whole population, including minorities (such as rights to same-sex marriage). The South African constitution is considered to be one of the most progressive in the world, incorporating elements from many others. And people have access to the vote.

But inclusion into merit-based job opportunities is already low, driven by limited access to education and social and environmental challenges. Bribery, clan-based thinking and nepotism exacerbate this inaccessibility.

The lack of perceived and actual inclusion to political and economic institutions was one of the triggers of the Arab Spring – oppressive regimes depriving their citizens of basic rights can trigger riots, which may lead to significant change. The Arab Spring was sparked by the suicide of a Tunisian vendor, triggering the protests that changed much of North Africa.

Inclusion, and exclusion respectively, can change in a short period of time, and the perception thereof even more rapidly. The effects are not identifiable by extrapolation only, as they can shake the very foundations of a society.

## Interdependencies of drivers

The 11 drivers described above are not fully independent of each other. Interdependencies and correlations exist between them. The experts and sounding board on this project evaluated these qualitatively and classified then as low, medium, and high. A quantitative assessment is not feasible due to the nature of the data.

For example, the interdependency of demography on number of jobs is low. The number of jobs can develop independently of demographic changes, and vice versa. The impact of education on entrepreneurship is high. Improvements to teaching hard and soft skills at schools may create a greater entrepreneurial mindset, which will contribute to better outcomes for people.

Certain factors have more interdependencies than others. The driver with the highest interdependencies is perceived inclusion. Entrepreneurship, schooling, and skills have high interdependency scores as well. Drivers with low interdependencies are the number of available jobs, demography, migration, access, and the social and cultural environment.

The interdependencies do not explain how impactful each driver is when it comes to fostering youth employment. The driver of perceived inclusion, however, seems to have a special role as it has links to most other drivers.

## Prioritisation of employment drivers

Above we investigated the 11 drivers for youth employment with South Africa-specific subcategories and their interdependencies. In order to use these drivers to form scenarios, the two most relevant drivers need to be identified to span a two-by-two matrix that describes four scenarios. The remaining nine drivers will provide further context to the scenarios.

In order to prioritise the drivers, they are plotted according to their impact on youth employment in South Africa, and the likelihood of their appearance.

The first dimension, namely impact, describes the magnitude of youth employment that a single driver is capable of causing. Economic growth causes more employment than better health, for example.

The second dimension, uncertainty, describes the uncertainty of what the impact of this driver will have.

All drivers are tested according to two criteria:

• Is the driver likely to change from its trajectory?
• If it changes, how significant will the impact be?

It is unclear if the perception of belonging and access will have an impact on employment and if so, what. South Africans becoming increasingly unhappy with the social divide and corruption could revolt, bringing the economy down, which would hit job numbers too. Or the perceived inclusion may not have any influence on employment. This means the inclusion driver is characterised by high levels of uncertainty.

The board of experts gathered in the scenario sounding board decided on the placement of the drivers along the lines of impact and uncertainty. Each board member made their decisions individually and anonymously to ensure unbiased results. To then make the ratings comparable, they were first normalised per expert and then normalised per driver. The average of the expert opinions is then plotted on the axes.

For impact, the *number of jobs* driver is ranked highest at 82.4 percent, with *migration,* at 34.1 percent, ranked lowest. The highest variance – experts not agreeing on the positioning – is for *perceived inclusion,* the lowest is for *skills.*

For uncertainty, the driver *perceived inclusion* is ranked highest at 69.8 percent, and *demography* the lowest at 19.1 percent. The leader in variance is *health* while *structural barriers* is at the bottom of the list.

*Number of available jobs* and *perceived inclusion* are listed as the main drivers for the 2040 scenarios.

Both dimensions combined allow for a scatter diagram. This diagram can be split into four fields: (1) the top right field with high impact and high uncertainty, (2) the two fields with high impact and low uncertainty, (3) low impact and high uncertainty, and lastly (4) the field with low impact and low uncertainty. The first field contains highly relevant drivers, which are, however, neither the most impactful nor most uncertain drivers, viz.: *skills,* *schooling*, *environment*, and *barriers*.

The drivers *perceived inclusion* and *health* are close to each other. It therefore is questionable to clearly prioritise *perceived inclusion* over *health*. However, the high variance of expert rankings for *health* compared to the low variance of *perceived inclusion* is an indicator for the confidence of the experts on the uncertainty of the driver.

## Bibliography

Acemoglu, D., & Robinson, J. A. (2013). *Why nations fail: The origins of power, prosperity, and poverty* (Internat. ed.). New York, NY: Crown Business.

AFP (2018). *South Africa economy grows 1.3% in 2017, beats expectations*. Daily Maverick.

Allianz (2020). *Global wealth report 2020*. Allianz.

Altbaker, A., & Bernstein, A. (2017). *No country for young people: The crisis of youth unemployment and what to do about it*. Johannesburg: CDE.

ARTE (Producer). & Aubry, E. (Director) (2017). *Mit offenen Karten*. Migration in Afrika (online).

Asche, H. (2015). Down to earth again: The third stage of African growth perceptions. *Africa Spectrum, 50*(3), 123–138.

Aspen Network of Development Entrepreneurs (2017). *South Africa's entrepreneurial ecosystem map*. Aspen Network.

Atkinson, A. B. (1998). Social exclusion, poverty and unemployment. In J. Hills (Ed.), *Exclusion, employment and opportunity* (pp. 1–20). London: London School of Economics and Political Science.

Balliester, T., & Elsheikhi, A. (2018). The future of work a literature review. *ILO Research Department Working Paper, 29*.

Basardien, F., Friedrich, C., & Parker, H. (2013). The relationship between planning strategies and entrepreneurial success for start-up entrepreneurs in the Western Cape. *The International Journal of Entrepreneurship and Innovation, 14*(4), 281–288.

Bava, S., & Tapert, S. F. (2010). Adolescent brain development and the risk for alcohol and other drug problems. *Neuropsychology Review, 20*(4), 398–413.

Bernstein, A. (2016). *Jobs: The growth agenda*. Priorities for mass employment and inclusion. Johannesburg: CDE.

Bernstein, A. (2017). *Teacher professional standards for South Africa: The road to better performance, development and accountability?* Johannesburg: CDE.

Bhorat, H., Cassim, A., Kanbur, R., Stanwix, B., & Yu, D. (2016). Minimum wages and youth: The case of South Africa. *Journal of African Economies, 25*, 61–102.

Bischoff, C., & Maree, J. (2017). Public sector unions in COSATU. In A. Bezuidenhout & M. Tshoaedi (Eds.), *Labour beyond COSATU* (pp. 170–190). Johannesburg: Wits University Press.

Brand South Africa (2012). *Health care in South Africa.* [online].

Bridgestock, L. (2018). *How much does it cost to study in the US?* [online].

Business Tech (2017). South Africa has the highest data prices among Africa's biggest economies.

BusinessTech (2021a, January 10). How many South Africans now rely on social grants: 1996 vs 2020. *BusinessTech.*

BusinessTech (2021b, July 30). Government proposed additional #exit tax# n emigrating South Africans. *BusinessTech.*

Capazorio, B. (2017). *SA's demographics are set to cause an economic dilemma, Statistician General says.* Times Live.

Credit Suisse (2017). *Global wealth report.* Credit Suisse.

Crush, J. (2011). Diasporas of the south: Locating the African diaspora in Africa. In S. Plaza & D. Ratha (Eds.), *Diaspora for development in Africa* (pp. 55–78). Washington DC: The World Bank.

Department: Basic Education (2016). Report of the ministerial task team appointed by minister Angie Motshekga to investigate allegations into the selling of posts of educators by members of the teachers unions and departmental officials in provincial education departments.

Department of Higher Education and Training (2015). *Statistics on post-school education and statistics on post-school education and training in South Africa 2015.*

Department of Home Affairs (2014). *Critical skills* (Government Gazette No. 37716) (online).

Douglas, K. (2017). *Now that AB InBev has acquired SABMiller, here are its plans for Africa.* Retrieved from www.howwemadeitinafrica.com/now-ab-inbev-acquired-sabmiller-plans-africa/58643/

Ensor, L. (2021). Basic income grant 'will reduce poverty and hunger, but won't lead to growth'. *Business Day Newspaper* (26 October 2021).

FIN24 (2014). *More unions quit COSATU's exec body.* FIN24.

Friedman, M. (1957). The permanent income hypothesis. In M. Friedman (Ed.), *A theory of the consumption function* (pp. 20–37). Princeton, NJ: Princeton University Press.

Friedman, M. (1962). *Capitalism and freedom.* Chicago, IL: University of Chicago press.

Gal, S., & Loudenback, T. (2018). *How much it costs to grab a pint of beer around the world.* Business Insider.

Gallie, D., Paugam, S., & Jacobs, S. (2003). Unemployment, poverty and social isolation: Is there a vicious circle of social exclusion? *European Societies, 5*(1), 1–32.

Gapminder (2021). *Gapminder tools.* [online].

Graham, L., & Lannoy, A. de (2016). *Youth unemployment: What can we do in the short run?* Econ3x3 [online].

Henry, J. P., Stephens, P. M., & Schaefer, K. E. (1977). *Stress, health, and the social environment: A sociobiologic approach to medicine (N). Topics in environmental physiology and medicine.* New York, NY: Springer.

ILO (2018). *Gender and employment.* ILO Publications (online).

IMF (2015). *Regional economic outlook, Sub-Saharan Africa. World economic and financial surveys.* Washington DC: International Monetary Fund.

Indeed (2018). *Entry level engineer salaries in the United States.* Econ3x3.

IRR (2016). *South African survey 2017.* Johannesburg: South African Institute of Race Relations.

Jernigan, D. (2013). Why South Africa's proposed advertising ban matters. *Addiction, 108*(7), 1183–1185.

Johnston, S., Spurrett, D., & Bernstein, A. (2011). *Reforming healthcare in South Africa: What role for the private sector?* Johannesburg: Centre for Development and Enterprise.

Khuluvhe, M. (2021). *Fact sheet: Adult illiteracy in South Africa.* Department: Higher Education and Training (online).

Kok, P., & Collinson, M. (2006). *Migration and urbanisation in South Africa. Report.* Pretoria: Statistics South Africa.

Kolvereid, L. (1996). Prediction of employment status choice intentions. *Entrepreneurship Theory and Practice, 21*(1), 47–58.

Lamrabat, A. (2009). Creating an inclusive society: Draft paper.

Leon, P. (2018). *Land expropriation without compensation: SA risks breaching international law, being massively sued.* Herbert Smith Freehills.

Levitas, R. (2005). *The inclusive society?: Social exclusion and new labour* (2nd ed.). London: Palgrave Macmillan UK.

Mahajan, S. (2014). *Economics of South African townships: Special focus on Diepsloot.* The World Bank (online).

Mahlakoana, T. (2018). *Oxfam urges South Africa to reduce widening wealth gap.* Business Day.

May, J. (2016). *Why child malnutrition is still a problem in South Africa 22 years into democracy.* The Conversation [online].

McGaughey, E. (2018). Will robots automate your job away? Full employment, basic income, and economic democracy. *Centre for Business Research Working Paper, 496.*

McKinsey Global Institute (2018). Notes from the Frontier: Modelling the impact of AI on the world economy. *Discussion Paper.*

Monga, C. (2018, September). *The role of the state in the dynamics of structural change.* Wits Business School.

Musterd, S., & Andersson, R. (2006). Employment, social mobility and neighbourhood effects: The case of Sweden. *International Journal of Urban and Regional Research, 30*(1), 120–140.

My Broadband (2021, August 26), South African grant recipients increased from 3 million to 18 million – and growing fast. *My Broadband online news, 26*

Naude, P. (2018, August). *Education and youth employment: A priority for all South Africans.* Johannesburg: GIBS.

Nxasana, S. (2018, August). *Education and youth employment: A priority for all South Africans.* GIBS, Johannesburg.

Paine, T. (1795). *The age of reason: Part the second. Being an investigation of true and of fabulous theology.* Paris: HD Symonds.

Rankin, N., & Roberts, G. (2011). Youth unemployment, firm size and reservation wages in South Africa. *South African Journal of Economics, 79*(2), 128–145.

Reddy, V., Bhorat, H., Powell, M., Visser, M., & Arends, A. (2016). *Skills supply and demand in South Africa.* Human Sciences Research Council.

Schirmer, S., & Bernstein, A. (2017). *Business, growth and inclusion: Tackling youth unemployment in cities, towns and townships.* Johannesburg: CDE.

Schwab, K. (2016). *The fourth industrial revolution: What it means, how to respond.* World Economic Forum.

Scott, K. M., Koenen, K. C., King, A., Petukhova, M. V., Alonso, J., Bromet, E. J., & Lee, S. (2018). Post-traumatic stress disorder associated with sexual assault among women in the WHO world mental health surveys. *Psychological Medicine, 48*(1), 155–167.

Singh, A. R., & Singh, S. A. (2008). Diseases of poverty and lifestyle, well-being and human development. *Mens Sana Monographs, 6*(1), 187–225.

Solomon, G., Frese, M., Friedrich, C., & Glaub, M. (2013). Can personal initiative training improve small business success? *The International Journal of Entrepreneurship and Innovation, 14*(4), 255–268.

South African Government (2021). *Old age pension.* [online].

South African Qualifications Authority (2010). National Qualifications Framework Act 67 of 2008.

Statistics South Africa (2021). *Quarterly labour force survey: (2nd quarter 2021).*

Stevens, P. (2004). *Diseases of poverty and the 10/90 gap.* London: International Policy Network.

Tanner, M. (2015). *The pros and cons of a guaranteed national income.* Washington DC: Cato Institute.

The Economist (2016, January 23). Future of work: Generation uphill. *The Economist.*

The Economist (2017a, August 26). The future of work: The human cumulus. *The Economist.*

The Economist (2017b, September 21). Freed enterprise: Psychology beats business training when it comes to entrepreneurship. *The Economist.*

The Economist (2018a, April 26). The lapsing of Finland's universal basic income trial: Plenty of UBI trials are under way, with more to come. *The Economist.*

The Economist (2018b, August 25). Tragedy of the commons: Land reform in South Africa has been slow and inept. It could get even worse. *The Economist.*

The Economist (2019a, February 16). Cyril Ramaphosa's light-bulb moment: How South Africa should tackle corruption. *The Economist.*

The Economist (2019b, February 16). Muck, meet shovel: Cyril Ramaphosa has made uneven progress in repairing South Africa. *The Economist.*

The Economist (2020, July 18). Measuring the poverty pandemic: Covid-19 has throttled South Africa's economy. *The Economist.*

The Economist (2021a, July 15). Jacob's looters: South Africa reels form the worst violence since apartheid. *The Economist.*

The Economist (2021b, September 22). Not so black and white: Unpicking inequality in South Africa. *The Economist.*

Thomas, G. (1997). Inclusive schools for an inclusive society. *British Journal of Special Education, 24*(3), 103–107.

UNICEF (2017). *Child and maternal health: South Africa.* [online].

United Nations (2017). *World population prospects 2017.* [online].

WHO (2014). *Global status report on alcohol and health, 2014.* Geneva: World Health Organization.

Witt, E. D. (2010). Research on alcohol and adolescent brain development: Opportunities and future directions. *Alcohol (Fayetteville, N.Y.), 44*(1), 119–124.

Wolfskämpf, V. (2016). *Jugendarbeitslosigkeit: Auf der Suche nach der richtigen Arbeit.* Deutschlandfunk.

World DataBank (2021). GDP growth (annual in %) – South Africa. [online].

World Population Review (2019). *World city populations 2019.* [online].

Yehuda, R. (2002). Post-traumatic stress disorder. *The New England Journal of Medicine, 346*(2), 108–114.

Z.a.zen Consulting (2017). *Entrepreneurship pamphlet.* Johannesburg: Z.a.zen Consulting.

Expert interviews

Participating observations

# 6 Youth employment scenarios for South Africa in 2040

Scenarios help to understand how the future might look. They do not aim to describe the most likely case that may present itself, but the extreme cases that hold possibilities. The most likely future setting is supposed to be between the extremes. Describing possible future states based on academically derived drivers and the extrapolation of these drivers, rather than the extrapolation of the status quo, does not provide any certainty for the scenarios, but merely an approximation of what is possible.

The following scenarios are set in South Africa in the year 2040. This might seem to be a long time ahead. From 2022, this is 18 years in the future. A child born now will only just enter the job market in 2040. An 18-year-old youth today will just have exited the youth bracket at 35 and will have found a status in life on which to build his or her adulthood, family, and future.

To put this timeframe in relationship to the past, we look at what happened 18 years ago. South Africa had four presidents in the last 18 years. Thabo Mbeki was in office from 1999 and served until 2008, when Kgalema Motlanthe served for less than a year and Jacob Zuma replaced him in 2009. In 2018, Zuma resigned, under pressure from the ruling party. The party replaced him with Cyril Ramaphosa who was later elected as president by the same party after it won the 2019 elections, enabling it to select the country's president. In South Africa, the winning party, rather than the electorate, decides on who is to be president.

To establish the most radical scenarios, the two main drivers – "number of available jobs" and "perceived inclusion" – are plotted on orthogonal axes. These are the most impactful as the $y$-axis and the most uncertain as the $x$-axis. As a result, there are four fields with the middle intersection of the axis reflecting the status quo.

DOI: 10.4324/9781003186052-7

The other nine drivers account for further relevant dimensions, although these are not geometrically illustrated. Over the next 18 years, the status quo can move in any direction, depending on the "pull" of each driver (see Figure 6.1).

The four fields above account for the four scenarios outlined in this chapter. They are:

- Scenario 1: Incorporates job growth but a decrease in perceived inclusion.
- Scenario 2: More jobs and a perception of improved inclusion.
- Scenario 3: Relative job losses combined with perceptions of improved inclusion.
- Scenario 4: Declining jobs and perceived inclusion.

These scenarios are named after the four seasons. Their content reflects attributes associated with these seasons and thus they are named *Spring*, *Summer*, *Fall* (autumn), and *Winter.*

Scenario 1, *Spring*, describes a potential South African spring, following the theme of the Arab Spring. Scenario 2, *Summer*, lets bright sunlight shine on the youth employment situation in 2040, when jobs are numerous and seem accessible. Scenario 3, *Fall*, reflects the fall of

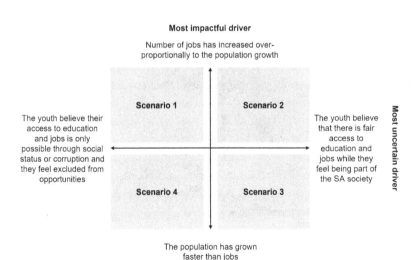

*Figure 6.1* Scenario matrix applied.

the economy and a reduction of jobs but also reflects the removal of excessive bureaucracy and lower levels of inequality. Lastly, Scenario 4, *Winter*, describes a season of despair, in which the economy has collapsed, and the youth has become resigned to its fate. In the last scenario, South Africa in 2040 is in a similar state to that of Zimbabwe in the early 21st century, with its once flourishing economy having crumbled (Figure 6.2).

The four scenarios were discussed, challenged, and iterated by the project's Sounding Board – a key element of the strategic conversation in the process of building scenarios. The aim was to make all scenarios plausible and internally constant, while at the same time not biased towards any one of them. Each outcome is as likely as another, covering possible future states at the extremes. This was achieved in the second session of the Sounding Board.

Each scenario is introduced below with a short narrative that is inspired by the fieldwork conducted in townships across South Africa. The narrative contextualises and illustrates the scenarios by providing an insight into the life of the fictional character of Lesedi, who was identified in Chapter 4 as being the average unemployed South African, and her family.

*Figure 6.2* The four seasons in 2040.

## Scenario 1 – Spring: The South African version of the Arab Spring

*Lesedi's uncle enters the dimly lit room. She looks up from her phone, which she has just been checking for the most recent news on social media. He stops and looks at her sitting at a table on which she has spread out a cloth and has just started painting large capital letters onto the white linen. He hands her something and whispers: "Here, take that." He turns his head towards the dark corner of the room where Thabo is sleeping. "Don't let them do to you what they did to your brother." Thabo has been sleeping a lot on that mattress in the corner since last week.*

*Last week, Thabo marched to Sandton, Johannesburg's alternative main business district, which is described by advertisers as "the richest square mile in Africa." His eyes were on fire before he left: "We will take what's ours, our share of what they have." He was desperate, having finished matric, but not having good enough grades to go to university. He was told to start a course at a TVET college. But that was far, too far. Hardly any of their graduates finds a job.*

*Thabo decided not to go anymore. He wanted to go to university and get a proper job; to become rich. That, however, seemed further away than ever. Now, he still looks bad. They had already reached Sandton where the stock exchange is situated, but there was plundering on the way, windows smashed, and cars set alight. Police watched, overwhelmed, but private security forces pushed back. First, they fired teargas, then rubber bullets. They beat up anyone they could get their hands on. Thabo was at the wrong place at the wrong time. Brutally beaten up, he was brought home by friends. Everyone knows that public hospitals do not have capacity. Private hospitals are only for the rich, and they are protected by private security.*

*Lesedi's uncle reaches into the pocket of his coat and reveals a small package. The light is shimmering and Lesedi only sees cloth held together with string. He hands it to her. Lesedi keeps holding it in her hands, seemingly surprised by its weight while her uncle turns around to exit the room. He stops and mumbles, "Be strong, stay safe," before he leaves.*

*Lesedi places the package next to the banner she is painting that reads "IT'S OURS" and unwraps it to find a loaded revolver.*

### The society

South African society is classist: there is a controlling and extremely wealthy elitist black class in the form of business owners and executives; an educated but relatively small middle class, in the form of managers

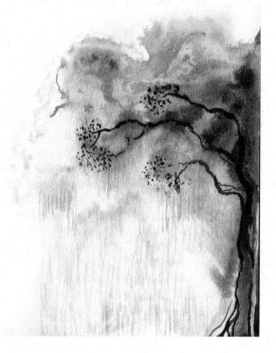

*Figure 6.3* Scenario 1 – Spring: The South African version of the Arab Spring.

and white-collar workers; and a poor lower class, some educated, some uneducated – basically all unemployed. Changing classes is practically impossible.

Key drivers are economic growth in services and capital-intensive industries paired with a rapid introduction of artificial intelligence that is making blue-collar workers dispensable. Opportunities for the lower class are close to zero. This group has been growing over-proportionally as families produce children to provide for the family later in life.

Jobs are inaccessible and require higher education levels. Education, particularly a university education, is necessary for to work in service industries, particularly in the new technology era. Although university education is provided for free, access to it is limited, as universities have implemented high barriers to entry.

Youth born into the lower class can access skills training and education, which provides them with practical skills. However, they are not absorbed into the labour market in high numbers. The social circumstances of school dropouts mean most do not pursue any further education. Consequently, youth unemployment is very high, at about two-thirds on average. It is nearly 100 percent among youth in the lower class, who are jobless regardless of whether or not they have spent many years in the educational system, have skills, or whether they dropped out of school.

In recent years, desperate youths have revolted by marching on governmental institutions. Protests have been peaceful at first, with scattered and disorganised violence. Acts of violence, signalling their helplessness, has been met with high levels of violence by the police and military, who start forcefully locking down townships and preventing the lower-class population from moving freely.

The state forces are not able to enclose the masses that now have practically shut down normal functioning in the city. The wealthy middle and upper class stay in their heavily guarded homes or get escorted by security forces or private security when they do go out. Protests spread across the country in an effort to get the government to resign. The South African version of the Arab Spring has erupted, triggered by unemployed and desperate youth.

### *Number of jobs*

Despite the rising protests and threat to middle-class normality, South Africa has managed to attract international investment, with companies attracted by the high standard of living alongside the comparably low cost of living, combined with lower costs for white collar workers. First- and second-tier cities benefit the most, leaving rural areas untouched. The investment is mostly into the services sector, already the predominant economic sector, creating jobs mostly in white-collar professions. However, due to the worsening safety situation, this trend is cooling off and international companies have started to repatriate their expatriate workers from South Africa.

The low skilled, mostly blue-collar, jobs are being replaced by machines and artificial intelligence, making it even more difficult for low-skilled workers to find a job and make a living. Industries most affected are labour intensive sectors, such as automotive manufacturing, mining, and farming.

The attractive and most well-paid jobs are in city centres and decentralised urban nodes such as Sandton. They are most accessible to the educated and wealthy, with the majority excluded by high suburban rentals and long distances to work.

### Perceived inclusion

The divide between rich and poor is widening, with socioeconomic status, rather than race or ethnicity, being the driver of social dynamics. The middle class has moved far out of reach for low-income families with poor education. Even empowerment schemes such as Broad-based black economic empowerment (B-BBEE) mostly give advantages to the established black elite, who benefit from well-paid jobs and equity transfers. The poor benefit little from empowerment initiatives, getting left further and further behind.

### Entrepreneurship

The lack of opportunities for low skilled workers has created a wave of one-person businesses, offering low-cost, low-skill services such as cooking, cleaning, or washing. Most businesses are in townships or reach into the formal economy, although many are not formally registered and not part of the tax base.

However, demand is relatively low and most fail to grow even while providing some sort of income to their founders.

### Demography

The demographic dividend starts to yield results. The poor still give birth to many children as a "retirement insurance," while the middle- and upper class have fewer children. Thus, the growing – and employed – middle class and upper income groups continue to fund social grants for the poor, but they also have to work into old age, as grants are limited and not sufficient to retain a healthy lifestyle. The life expectancy of the middle and upper classes has improved, while the poor live about 10 years less, on average.

### Migration patterns

The influx of foreigners has decreased as the economic situation in neighbouring countries has improved, providing job opportunities to their citizens and stemming the tide of emigration to South Africa, although xenophobic attacks have increased in low-income areas of South Africa against those who remain. Increasing nationalism has led to fewer critical skills visas being issued and a strong push to local content and employing local staff.

The embedded nepotism among the black elites and job reservation in the name of empowerment of previously disadvantaged South Africans has led to mass emigration of educated and skilled white South Africans out of the country, who have sought opportunities in other regions.

### Schooling

The quality of education has improved, reflecting international standards but this has driven a wedge between the more and less educated strata of society. Teacher training has not kept up with these improvements, perpetuating the previous divide between a minority of high-performing students and a majority of underperforming children, many of whom are dropping out of the system before they matriculate.

The gap between private and public schools is still marked. Middle- and upper-class parents send their children to private schools with well-trained and non-unionised teachers. The lower class sends its children to public schools, where teachers can provide the support that is needed for more pupils to reach their matric year.

Students are pushed out of the schooling system when they fail, enforcing the lower-class misery of no education, no skills, and no prospects. However, TVET colleges take in dropouts and provide them with the opportunity to learn manual trades.

### Skills development

The quality of skills development improves, with the inclusion of more practical content in the school curriculum, offering an apprenticeship-like education. The pass rates are high, but the placement rates are low, as employer needs are not sufficiently incorporated in the design and intake to the programmes, leaving even educated youth jobless.

Access to universities is limited. Tertiary education is free, but as consequence, the universities have increased their academic barriers to entry, reducing the number of admitted students as a result of budget restrictions. Consequently, highly qualified middle- and upper-class students tend to be the ones who are accepted by universities, who could, but do not need to, pay fees. This mechanism enforces social division.

### Health

The class divides in the society are also reflected in the health system. The rich benefit from an expensive private health system, and are healthy, living longer, while the poor do not have access to advanced medical treatment and are forced to use underfinanced public facilities. As a result, health in low-income families continues to be poor.

### Access

The classist society has also left its footprint on social access and housing: the poor live far from business centres in cities and lack proximity to jobs, while access is undermined by high transport costs and traffic congestion. Remoteness of work opportunities from homes is the main barrier to finding a job.

IT skills have improved as data and airtime have become cheaper, providing easier access to job searches. However, most jobs are not advertised, or are not accessible without knowing the right people and having the relevant political contacts. Nepotism and corruption are rampant.

### Employability barriers

Unions have steadily lost their influence as the number of low-skilled and unionised workers decreases. Subsidies are being abused to cut the cost of labour to companies who are not incentivised to create new jobs or ease entry to employment for inexperienced and often unqualified youth. Preference is given to older and more experienced workers.

### Social and cultural environment

The social fabric of families remains damaged, with one in ten children not growing up with both parents. The socialisation regarding family, peers, school, and media is very much dependent on the social status of the environment, to which the young people are exposed. Alcohol and drugs are consumed regularly in precarious environments to "escape" the daily misery of life. Money to get by is often acquired illegally, and often through violence. Crime rates are higher than ever.

## Scenario 2 – Summer: Fair access to a high number of jobs

*It's Lesedi's first night back in South Africa. She sits in her room and enjoys the silence. It is the first time there is no sound since she landed. First, she arrived at the airport and her family picked her up, then they had a big dinner. Everybody came and wanted to hear her stories. She sits at her desk and thinks back to the magnitude of overwhelming* experiences. *Just two-and-a-half years ago, she applied for a scholarship with a big Chinese technology company. She got accepted and started studying advanced analytics in Johannesburg in a globally competitive programme. The company that pays her scholarship also funds the study programme.*

*After just one year at university, she was asked to intern at her sponsoring company's headquarters in Chengdu, China. She enjoyed her time a great deal, although it was her first time abroad. The Mandarin she had learnt in high school helped her to make friends quickly and feel welcome. After just one more semester in Johannesburg, Lesedi was offered the opportunity to study a term abroad in Shanghai at the best-rated university worldwide for data analytics, fully funded by her sponsor. The last half-year was tough for her, as she missed her family and had to work long hours to stay on top of the assignments. Lesedi looks up, also thinking of the good memories she had been able to collect as a result of being resilient and not giving up on her dreams.*

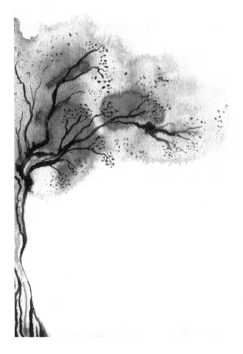

*Figure 6.4* Scenario 2 – Summer: Fair access to a high number of jobs.

*She looks to the corner of the room where her brother's bed stands. He was not at the airport, nor at the family dinner. She misses her brother. Thabo is in Cape Town at a TVET college, being trained in mechatronics. Talented young people with an understanding of robotics and the skills to maintain artificial intelligence production sites are rare. The government has shifted TVET education towards the needs of the corporate sector.*

*Being relieved of the stress, the buzz around her, and all the experiences she accumulated, she shivers, and then smiles. The internship and the term abroad made her eligible to work for her sponsor as soon as she finishes her honour's degree. She found the contract in her mail when she got home today. She and her brother will be the first ones in the family to start working in a well-paid job right after finishing their education. She knows her family is very proud.*

### The society

Economic growth has narrowed the social divide between rich and poor and millions of new jobs have been created, making opportunities egalitarian and ubiquitous.

The key drivers here are improved governance and housing reforms, which are driven by the influence of China. The Chinese government has increased its influence in Africa as it has in other regions. It has charmed many African governments, including that in South Africa, by offering lucrative trade deals and preferential infrastructure financing. Ideological similarities between the ruling African National Congress (ANC) and the Chinese Communist Party, paired with the economic success of China, have lured the South African government to seek engagement with Asia rather than the previous colonisers in the Western world.

The South African government has addressed corruption and improved bureaucratic processes significantly, attracting foreign investors and boosting the domestic market. Housing reform, which is a key part of the ANC's land reform, now gives South Africans the chance to own a government house in a township or receive a subsidised rental to live in middle-class suburbs in a system that is similar to that employed by Singapore's model of mixing government and private housing to break up racial and class tensions. These and other reforms have led to middle-class growth and improving living standards among poor people.

Education, particularly job readiness, has improved, as mandatory practical work in the form of internships and apprenticeships has been implemented in schools, TVETs, and universities.

The youth unemployment rate has dropped to 15 percent. In urban areas, the youth can find jobs easily, although it remains a challenge in rural areas.

## Number of jobs

The country has left its long period of economic recession behind and confidence in the South African economy has returned. Wealth has slowly but surely democratised, making social progression a reality for many on the back of increased investment. Consequently, the middle class has grown and become a driver of local demand for goods and services.

Millions of new jobs have been created as a result of the development of special economic zones in secondary cities, while other programmes have led to jobs being created in townships and rural areas, bringing relief to areas that had been the most affected by unemployment, crime, and despair.

## Perceived inclusion

The people use their vote to improve change governance, penalising poor behaviour and nepotism, which has helped to drive compliance by officials in politics and administration. Youth voting participation is high.

There has been some social unrest on the back of slow delivery of promises by a new president after an initial period of post-election expectations. However, over time, there have been continuous, albeit slow, improvements, which led changed peoples' mindsets and led to more positive behaviour and a greater adherence to the rule of law.

Tertiary education at TVETs and universities is now free for the poor, while a loan system has also improved the participation among the lower middle classes in these institutions.

The access to jobs is now mostly merit based, driven by an improved education system and a less onerous B-BBEE empowerment policy.

## Entrepreneurship

A government-led initiative supported by business and NGOs has helped to develop the confidence of unemployed youth to start their own business and generated linkages between existing and new businesses.

Even though many of the new owner-run businesses succeed, the increased exposure to business through self-employment increases the work-readiness of people significantly, making it easier for those who have taken the initiative to start a business to later find a corporate job or start a new company. The growing entrepreneurial start-up culture helps to create jobs incrementally.

### Demography

The demographic dividend is paying off. High taxation and a large working age population, combined with relatively high employment, allow support the elderly and the continuation of grants and subsidies for the disadvantaged. Life expectancy has increased slightly due to improving health of the population, but also as a result of improved access to health services on the back of a general health insurance and better public health facilities.

The retirement age has risen along with increased life expectancy, enabling a healthy ratio of working to non-working people.

Increased trust in government institutions has caused the fertility rate to drop from 2.3 to two, as people become less reliant on children as their retirement insurance. This stabilises the size of the population.

### Migration patterns

The economic upturn has lured South Africans back from the diaspora, particularly in the medical sector. The growing local talent pool has made it more difficult for foreigners to get a critical skills visa but has improved service delivery in South Africa.

The economic uplift and good governance have spilled over into neighbouring Zimbabwe, where improved governance and economic opportunities have attracted many Zimbabweans from South Africa, decreasing the potential for xenophobic violence and improving business and job opportunities for South Africans.

### Schooling

The schooling system has been reformed. Teachers are better educated and have to adhere to strict performance measures that are strictly enforced. Primary schools now teach in local African languages, increasing children's and parents' participation. Public schools increase their performance by accessing corporate funding, incentivised through revised empowerment programmes. Unions were strong-armed to comply in order not to close underperforming public schools.

School dropout rates have improved, as most students now stay in school and finish matric in Grade 12, while matric pass rates improve. Mandatory internships are introduced, exposing students to the working environment while building the soft skills needed for employment.

The quality gap of education between rural and urban areas, and particularly between private and public schools, is still significant. Rural schools do not receive the private funding urban schools do, and well-educated teachers prefer living and working in urban areas.

### Skills deployment

Centres of specialisation, an adaption of the German dual apprenticeship and schooling system, have been rolled out aggressively. These centres are now the main alternative to universities and also accept school dropouts, allowing them to find a different educational path to employment.

These training programmes are now distinctly more driven by employer demand than before. Companies sponsor learnerships for the jobs they need and hire most of the students, while training providers are compensated on a pay-for-performance mechanism, incentivising their alignment with youth and employers.

### Health

Government has strengthened health education in poorer areas, emphasising nutrition and preventative healthcare methods. More pro-active health management has helped to decrease the rate of HIV, tuberculosis, and malnutrition. As a result, there are fewer families headed by children, allowing more youth to continue in education, thereby reducing health-related dropout rates.

The public healthcare system has improved with the introduction of a general public health insurance with an increase in clinics around the country. Both have resulted in a sharp increase in patient treatments, reducing the waiting times for patients to be seen by a doctor and the time to cure illnesses, ultimately reducing illness-based absenteeism from work and school.

### Access

Housing reform has stipulated that all new urban developments accommodate different income groups. A minimum of 10 percent of apartments in each complex are allocated to low-income families. This has reduced the social divide, and particularly the travel times to work and associated costs.

IT literacy has improved due to better schooling, allowing for easier access to opportunities listed on the internet. Non-governmental organisations such as Harambee train and prepare young people for job readiness on a large scale across the country, including in remote areas.

Social ties still account for a fair share of job placements. However, new trends such as the housing reforms, mean social ties now extend beyond clans, ethnicities, and income.

### *Employability barriers*

Subsidies have become more targeted and are focused on education and work-readiness, rather than being used to supplement wages. Unions are still powerful. However, due to the improved economic situation, they have become more cooperative and supportive of the changing skills demand.

Due to improved job access, hiring and firing has become easier, improving the willingness of companies to hire more quickly, and in greater numbers. This creates entry opportunities at all skill levels and opens doors, particularly for the unskilled.

As South African skills development has become state-of-the-art, and incorporates practical training, companies now focus on hiring from TVETs and universities directly, rather than solely focusing on experienced workers, thereby creating opportunities for younger workers.

### *Social and cultural environment*

There are now more "intact" families with two parents. This and the improved social inclusion have decreased stress levels, allowing youth to focus on education. In line with the above, substance abuse has been reduced due to government initiatives, educating youth and parents about the side effects and curbing production and trade.

Women now play a stronger role in South African society. They have become the better students and stay in the educational system as long as men, leading to similar opportunities and pay for comparable jobs.

### Scenario 3 – Fall: The number of jobs has declined but access is fair

*Lesedi leans on her desk and looks up. The candle casts dancing shadows on her face. She still has more than a dozen pages to go through before her test tomorrow.*

*She is tired, and her tummy rumbles. The last time she ate at was lunch-time. After her father lost his job a year ago, she and her family suffered more hardship. Now everybody gets a basic income, a policy the unions have pushed through as a result of the spectre of massive job layoffs. Corporations have moved quickly into automation in South Africa, and, as local labour is expensive, they have exploited cheaper manual labour from neighbouring countries. Even though the basic income is better than no income, it is too little to sustain a family with no one working. Thabo, her brother, has started to work in construction. He did well in his matric and started a vocational training course as a builder. He could graduate early, as Lesedi supported him while studying, and their father worked. Now that he has lost his job, Thabo has started to work sooner than planned and he was lucky to have found a job.*

*Lesedi's father and brother share their basic income with the family to allow Lesedi to continue her studies, while still putting food on the table. Lesedi knows that the hopes of her family lie with her. She studies, so they believe she will get a good job. It is tough. The competition is stiff as everyone is looking for work.*

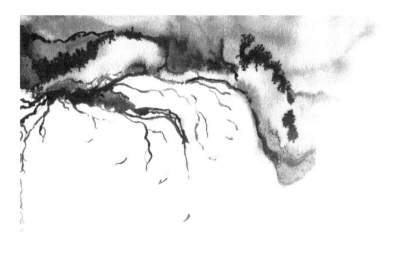

*Figure 6.5* Scenario 3 – Fall: The number of jobs has declined but access
is fair.

*Lesedi takes a deep breath and focuses her attention again on the remaining pages. Tomorrow's test is crucial for her to get accepted to do her honour's degree. Without it, there is no chance of getting a job, and no chance of her helping her family.*

## The society

The economy has grown at a low, one-digit annual rate, just above stagnation, although the government has managed to improve social cohesion and cut down on red tape. Jobs are scarce as population growth outpaces the available work, while new technologies have reduced demand for human labour.

However, even though the economic growth is slow, tertiary education is now free, and the government has improved the schooling system. In addition, a universal basic income has been introduced as a reaction to low employment, replacing the social grant system and allowing the millions of unemployed people to participate in the economy, albeit at a low level.

The universities and TVET colleges have increased the proportion of on-the-job training and soft-skills development. This has resulted in a high job-readiness among tertiary graduates.

The available jobs are advertised and allocated according to merit and achievement, giving the qualified youth a preference over the more experienced but less educated older generation. This has caused the youth unemployment rate to drop, but the general unemployment rate to rise, both at about 35 percent. Barriers to employment have fallen, while opportunities have become merit based.

## Number of jobs

South Africa's growth continues to be one of the lowest on the continent. The interest in African countries from the West has waned, although fast-growing Asian countries continue to exploit Africa for their own economic advantage, particularly China.

International corporations have sought opportunities in Africa beyond South Africa, as these markets promise higher growth, more untapped opportunities, and more flexible and cheaper labour regimes.

Policies and politics in South Africa have become transparent and corruption has been eradicated due to the improved political environment, offering alternatives to frustrated voters. But as noted above, population growth has undermined the increase in available jobs that have been created as a result of the improved operating environment.

### Perceived inclusion

Fees at educational institutions have fallen. Government has reprioritised finances, making access to good education independent of social status. Schooling standards have improved. Now everyone can get decent education at primary, secondary, and tertiary levels. Even rural areas have been included in the uplift, supported by local language education.

Job placements are fair and merit-based, without corruption. Nevertheless, red tape and low availability of jobs result in long queues for work opportunities.

### Entrepreneurship

Incubation programmes try to attract local talent, but the funds to scale are lacking. One-person owned and run businesses come and go, without leaving a lasting mark on the economy or on the individual's pocket.

### Demography

The demographic dividend has not materialised. Fertility rates have remained constant as families continue to see children as social security for their retirement. The share of the working age population has declined, and the occupation rate is low. The retirement age remains at 65 to create opportunities for younger people.

### Migration patterns

As other African countries have experienced an economic boom, many African immigrants have returned to their home countries. Due to the high level of education and the opportunities elsewhere, there is a brain drain from all classes in society. This trend, however, does not affect the local economy, as there is sufficient talent available locally.

### Schooling

The government has focused on improving schools. A system of having dedicated exit points from high school, feeding into a dual education apprenticeship model, has significantly reduced dropout rates, and increased possible paths to employment. The matric results have improved, as teachers are being thoroughly assessed, improving the quality of classes and pass rates.

The gap between public and private schools has decreased as a result of improvements at public schools, including those in the rural areas.

### Skills deployment

The German model of a dual education, where classroom education and on-the-job training run parallel to each other, has been established, using centres of specialisation. The schools feed students into this system according to their preference and capabilities.

The access to these TVET colleges is fair and free, as the government and companies provide funds to run the training programmes in accordance with their qualitative and quantitative skills requirements. Still, the programmes' placement rates are not high, due to the low availability of jobs in the economy. The perception of vocational training as a pathway has improved, by integrating it into the schooling system.

### Health

The gap between the public and private systems is still large. Consequently, the poor are overly affected by diseases and illnesses. Due to the economy's poor performance, and the resulting strains on livelihoods, many children are malnourished.

### Access

The cost for finding a job has decreased as cell phone charges have dropped, and transportation fees have decreased, with the rollout of a widespread public bus system. IT literacy and access to the internet have improved, easing the search for opportunities advertised online.

Social ties have become less relevant in job searching, as all jobs have to be advertised and allocated based on merit. Cases of nepotism and corruption are investigated and have negative consequences for those involved.

### Employability barriers

Unions use their influence to ensure that jobs are advertised, and that recruitment is based on achievement and qualifications. Employers, however, still prefer older and unionised workers over young talent, who bring the skills sets required for the technological shift to automation.

Youth wage subsidies, in combination with the improved education, have helped to get more qualified youth into vacant jobs.

### Social and cultural environment

Only few families are "intact," that is, with two parents present. Violence in low-income neighbourhoods continues, as the government does not have the funds to finance substantial improvements in infrastructure and security. Many children suffer from ongoing stress.

Alcohol and drug abuse have increased slightly due to the higher overall unemployment leading to higher levels of desperation and violence.

Women's pay is now equal to that of men, but despite this, there are still fewer women participating in the workforce than men.

## Scenario 4 – Winter: Resignation of youth and economy

*Lesedi leans back in her armchair and looks around her room. The large windows overlook the Sandton skyline. She can only see the silhouettes of the modern skyscrapers and the well-rounded office buildings as the moon shines. The lights are out.*

*Lesedi stares out of the window and thinks of the old days, when she still shared a room with her brother in the little house in Soweto. She was excited about the change. She thinks about the joy and enthusiasm in her family when they moved north, to the lavish suburbs with their big houses. She was not sad about the white people leaving. She did not have any white or Indian, coloured or Asian friends, anyhow, so, she did not miss them. She also did not really understand why or how they left. Everyone was just talking about times changing for the better.*

*She remembers her father and brother jointly buying a new, large, German SUV at about the same time they moved. They were very proud. Lesedi's father was a bit worried about the loan he took out, but times looked good then. He was very happy when he was able to pay off his loan much faster than he had expected. The prices rose, but the loans did not, so it was easy to pay it off soon.*

*The same car is parked in the driveway. Lesedi cannot remember the last time it was used. It had been extremely difficult to source fuel for it. When her brother Thabo, who moves around the country taking care of law and order and making sure the change is still happening, comes back home, he brings a canister or two of fuel. They can take a ride through town and visit their family. But Thabo has not been home in a while. The last few times he came, he did not bring fuel. Now the car has been stationary for months.*

*Last time Thabo came home, he also looked frail, and slimmer than usual. He said that they did not get food regularly, and when they did, it was only small portions. Lesedi feels lucky having her extended family around, who takes care of them all. They all have large houses, with gardens where they can grow some vegetables. Her uncle even used to have some chickens, before the government reminded him of his duty towards his great nation. Lesedi also tried growing vegetables in their garden, but the soil seemed to be infertile. She remembers the days when supermarket shelves were full but they are long gone. Today, the shelves are empty, and the few goods they offer are imported and unaffordable.*

*Lesedi remembers Thabo complaining about a constant headache. Her father tried taking him to a doctor, but there was none who was willing to work for the little money they could afford. The public hospitals had long queues and it could take days just to get an appointment, or even some medicine. Finally, Lesedi's father found a traditional healer, but he was too far away. The walk would have taken a day.*

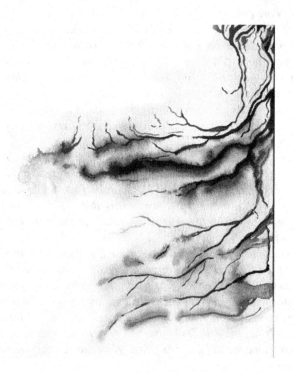

*Figure 6.6* Scenario 4 – Winter: Resignation of youth and economy.

*Lesedi lets her eyes wander across the room, her room, and for the first time, she asks herself who might have lived in this room before. When they moved in, her dad said the previous owners left, because the country was finally given back to its people. Lesedi asks herself if she might have been happier if she were still in their old house, having her brother and her family around, having a light bulb brightening her and Thabo's room, eating chicken off a metal plate, taking medicine if you were sick. This would have been better than owning a designer lamp but not having electricity, having porcelain plates but just a few raw vegetables to eat off them, and suffering from pain without the prospect of relief.*

### The society

The economy has imploded, and the currency has plummeted. Jobs are scarce. Inflation has skyrocketed. The educated professionals have emigrated.

The key driver of this scenario is radical redistribution on the back of the government's failure to grow the economy and improve governance. As a result of a loss of political support, the ruling party radicalised its policies, focusing specifically on converting the low-level land redistribution into a radical form of expropriation without compensation.

This new populist initiative did not only target vacant or unused land, but also arable productive farms, random urban houses, and even apartment blocks. Worst of all, large corporations, particularly in mining, chemical, energy, and financial services companies, were nationalised, with 51 percent of the shares taken by the government. The expropriation did not follow a comprehensible logic but seemed random, with nepotism and corruption appearing to played a major role.

International companies shut down all their local business. Jobs vanished by the thousands, daily. The wealthy packed their suitcases, and left the country, leaving behind a tiny existing and aspirant elite that was well positioned to leverage its political access to resources and political patronage. Those who could not afford to emigrate also remained. This was reminiscent of what had played out in countries such as Venezuela and in Zimbabwe some time before.

The educational and health system had become accessible to everyone but the budget to keep this afloat provide to be unsustainable, affecting the quality and viability of offerings in both sectors.

Unemployment among the youth had almost reached 100%, and opportunities for jobs seemed far off. Those who could sought jobs in politics, or abroad.

The country came to resemble Robert Mugabe's Zimbabwe, but with a lower level of education and less political violence, but much more violent petty crime.

## Number of jobs

The automotive, farming, and mining industries increased the levels of automation to improve competitiveness but also to avoid the cost and hassle associated with the increasing influence of and interference by trade unions. This has dramatically reduced the number of jobs in these previously labour-intensive sectors.

Bad governance and corruption led to disinvestment, with international companies concerned about reputational damage from compliance scandals in South Africa, which could put them in the line of fire of US and European regulators.

Increased bureaucracy and corruption, combined with a declining economy, has eradicated thousands of jobs. White- and blue-collar workers have been laid off, with little to no chance of finding a new job.

## Perceived inclusion

The mostly black elite is moving its money offshore to avoid high taxes and to mitigate the volatility of the local currency.

The children of wealthy families are sent abroad to schools and universities, creating a new South African diaspora overseas and in stable African countries. Those that choose or have to stay in South Africa are starting to get left behind. Social systems have collapsed. The country has achieved greater equality, but this has happened at the expense of quality health and education services, among others.

However, the elites have benefited from the expropriation, creating an ever-widening divide between themselves and a vast mass of desperate poor. The high levels of desperation have sparked protests that are often violently supressed by police.

Access to the few remaining jobs is limited and requires the right connections. Knowing the right people or paying them off is perceived to be the only feasible way to find work.

## Entrepreneurship

Even small businesses do not survive, as their market has collapsed due to lack of disposable income among potential clients. Cash is short, and the poor do not have bank accounts or cannot process card payments. There is no organised support from government for SMEs or start-ups.

## Demography

The demographic dividend has not been realised, as the share of working population to the unemployed is marginal. The trend towards an increase in life expectancy and a reduction in the fertility rate, due to better access to healthcare, has reversed in the wake of the near bankruptcy of the national healthcare system. The private healthcare system has deteriorated as middle-class incomes decline and those who can afford it travel abroad for medical care.

At this stage, the life expectancy is lower and fertility rates are higher than they were in 2018. The retirement age has increased, as those that have work have no social net for retirement and are not able to rely on their families because many of them also do not have jobs.

## Migration patterns

The educated middle class has left South Africa for jobs in the United Kingdom, the United States, Canada, Australia, and neighbouring countries in the region. Zimbabwe has seen a steep upward trajectory, catching up to where South Africa used to be, and it is attracting talent and investment from South Africa.

Increasing poverty has led to a rise in xenophobia, with South Africans feeling increasingly threatened by the presence of foreigners. The upsurge in violence against them has led many foreigners to emigrate or relocate.

## Schooling

The matric pass rate has remained low while dropout rates have increased. The gap between rural and urban, and between public and private education, remains large. Practical soft skills are not taught in schools, nor is training learners in life or entrepreneurial skills taking place.

## Skills development

As access to skills development in form of TVET colleges becomes free, there is an increase in learner numbers, which the institutions are unable to meet. As a result, the quality of the education, particularly among public TVETs, decreases, and their exposure to employer needs reduces.

The few jobs available can be filled inexpensively with the available unemployed, but sufficiently qualified, workforce.

Private TVETs that used to have more reputable programmes mainly close as their funding models, based on corporate B-BBEE investments, dry up.

### Health

The free and egalitarian National Health Insurance has been implemented, with the state absorbing the cost for anyone to go to any hospital or doctor. Consequently, the general health of the population has improved, although the broader economic decline has led many doctors to emigrate. The state insurance system has not been able to maintain its high standards. Eventually, the public health system sinks to levels lower than they were before the health system reform.

### Access

The few jobs that are available are not advertised and are given to family, friends, or political affiliates. Without a network there is no chance of finding an occupation.

The poor stay far from areas where the few jobs exist. Houses in suburban areas that the middle class once occupied are either vacant or run down. Transport and communications are expensive, as petrol prices have spiked, and telecoms providers have stopped investing in infrastructure due to regulatory issues and onerous bureaucracy. This has resulted in a drop in mobile phone and internet coverage and an increase in prices.

### Employability barriers

The influence of trade unions on politics and policies prevails, making it even harder for businesses to manoeuvre in turbulent economic times. Due to a high rate of unemployment, the employers can pick and choose the most qualified and experienced, mostly older, candidates for jobs. It is almost impossible for youth to find a merit-based occupation.

### Culture and social impact on youth

Desperation is high, causing substance abuse, and leading to domestic violence and lasting stress. There has not been any improvement in gender bias. Women get married even earlier to have children that might take care of them when they experience a crisis, even though those children are unlikely to find jobs in later life. Teenage pregnancy and high school dropout rates combined with general economic hardship means an increase in levels of desperation, often expressed through violence.

## Bibliography

Van der Heijden, K. (2005). *Scenarios: The art of strategic conversation.* Chichester; Hoboken, NJ: John Wiley.
Expert interviews
Participating observations

# 7 Charting a new path to youth employment

Supporting youth employment will not only build a positive trajectory for the *Summer* scenario and mitigate the risk of drifting towards the negative scenarios, but it is also the building block for a more equal society in South Africa today. This chapter discusses ongoing and new initiatives and proposals that have been derived from this research. All 11 drivers of youth unemployment listed in Chapter 5 need to be tackled in one way or another in order to address the jobs crisis in South Africa. These actions need to be complemented by various other programmes driven by either the public or private sector, or both in partnership.

## Existing initiatives for addressing youth unemployment

There are numerous youth employment interventions and programmes in action. Government, public–private partnerships, NGOs, schools, universities, and businesses have an interest in growing available work and jobs. Below is a snapshot of what is on offer in this regard, including both well-known and some lesser-known initiatives, as well as those with a unique approach. The overview does not claim to be exhaustive.

### YES4Youth

The Youth Employment Services (YES), or YES4Youth, is an employment programme initiated by the South African government. Top business leaders such as the former managing director of Goldman Sachs, Colin Coleman, and the former CEO of top financial services company Investec, Stephen Koseff, sit on the board of YES4Youth. It aims to provide work experience to one million young people. President Cyril Ramaphosa set youth employment as one of his key priorities, for which YES is the vehicle.

The idea is simple: companies pay the salaries of previously unemployed youths for one year, whether they work at the sponsoring

DOI: 10.4324/9781003186052-8

company, or at another business. The salary is set at the minimum wage of about R3,500 per month. The programme is set up for previously disadvantaged groups, and white South Africans are excluded from it. Participating companies benefit by having their broad-based black economic empowerment (B-BBEE) score increased by one or two levels.

The number of youths placed on the payroll depends on the sponsoring company's own headcount, average turnover for the past three years, or the average net profit after tax for the previous three years. The criterion with the highest result is used for the calculation. The programme admits candidates only for one year. By November 2021, about 1,700 companies had signed up, placing more than 66,000 youth in temporary employment since the programme was established in 2018.

The programme provides young people with workplace experience, helping them to find a subsequent job, either with the company offering the one-year job, or with another employer. However, it does not create new jobs, as this can only be driven by some form of growth or expansion, and there is a risk that the beneficiaries may be unemployed again after the year ends. If there had been the need for workers before the intervention, then the jobs would have been created without YES.

Still, participants do benefit from training and exposure to work, and from the redistribution of wealth from profitable or large corporations to unemployed individuals and families.

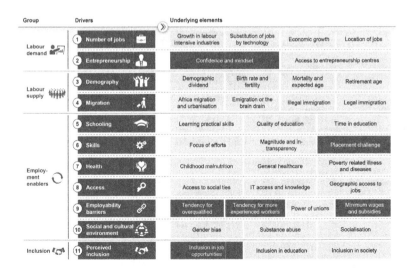

*Figure 7.1* YES' contribution to employment drivers.

### Harambee

Harambee is one of the largest bridging, work-readiness training, and placement programmes in South Africa supporting youth employment. Harambee is the Swahili phrase for "putting all together" and is a symbol of self-help. It was established in 2011 as an independent, not-for-profit social enterprise to work with individual businesses, government agencies, local and international donors, industry sector associations, youth-serving organisations, assessment specialists, behaviour change experts, and technology providers. Harambee aims to place young people with one or more of its 450 employer partners. The target market is previously disadvantaged South African youths who are unemployed and have not been permanently employed with one company for more than a year. They must have at least finished Grade 11, the grade before the final matric year. They are assessed and matched to a suitable employer. One of the benefits is being trained to apply for a job. Harambee also offers job-birding, where, for example, they train the youth to be on time, or to stand for long periods if they want to become cashiers.

Harambee has assessed 1.7 million young people and helped more than 50,000 to find their first job. It has built a broad ecosystem in an effort to link employers to young job seekers in order to boost its placement rates. However, these remain low, at less than 3 percent of the people on its books.

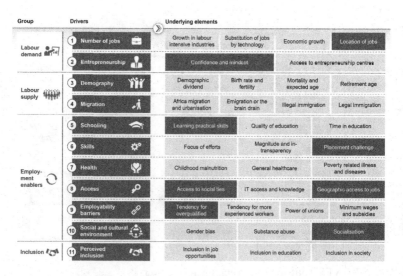

*Figure 7.2* Harambee's contribution to employment drivers.

## Placement agencies

South Africa does have a number of placement agencies specialising in entry-level jobs. They include CareerJunction, Giraffe, JobStarter, and Lulaway. These companies typically allow youths to register with their qualifications and link them to companies seeking workers.

## Bridging efforts

As established in the previous chapters, South Africa has a discrepancy between the education pupils receive and the needs of employers. There are organisations that bridge this gap. One of them is Bridge. It commits to engaging in learner support, early childhood development, teacher development, and school leadership. It achieves these aims by connecting people, driving collaboration, improving the quality of education, and sharing ideas.

Another organisation that aims to bridge the gap between youths' capabilities and employers' needs is the Maharishi Institute, which has a novel approach to the problem. As a non-profit tertiary institution, it helps disadvantaged youth to obtain a degree and, simultaneously, work experience. It does this by getting students to help with managing the organisation. This not only saves them money on overheads but also provides students with real-life challenges to tackle.

The institute has, through the screening it does of candidates on arrival, uncovered the fact that many young people in South Africa have post-traumatic stress disorder (PTSD) as a result of their challenges. Just those screened for acceptance at its facility show high levels of PTSD, with about 60 percent of females and 30 percent of males affected. Activities at the institute help to address this problem as participants have their days filled with education and management responsibilities, and they are able to leave their domestic issues at home and concentrate fully on self-development. The levels of PTSD decrease significantly as a result of this holistic approach to education, according to Taddy Blecher, the institute's founder.

SOS Children's Villages International, a globally active NGO supporting youth in precarious family situations, is also active in this space. It collaborated with large corporations such as global insurance company Allianz and logistics giant DHL to start YouthCan!, an initiative to support young people in their education-to-employment trajectory. The programme offers the youth the opportunity to get on-the-job experience through the SOS working environment. This appears to have a positive influence on their employability.

## Five proposals to tackle youth unemployment

The existing initiatives aiming at tackling youth unemployment in South Africa do support young people, but they do not support employment or job growth. While organisations help these individuals to improve their chances of finding a job, if they do get one, this means someone else loses out. The only way to effectively solve the problem is to create new jobs. It is this key issue that must be addressed. It is the most impactful driver for employment – perceived inclusion – that needs to be addressed in order to mitigate the risk of the country drifting into a *Spring* or *Winter* scenario.

This means that initiatives to drive employment must also create jobs. Ideally, economic growth should be in labour intensive industries. This needs to be underpinned by medium- to long-term economic policies focused on building productive capacity, international trust in the country, and technological development. However, South Africa's high levels of unionisation, weak skills base, onerous labour laws, and low levels of productivity have undermined its industrialisation trajectory. This has been exacerbated by a disconnect between the government and private sector, which is key to forging an industrial path. None of these issues is explicitly considered in employment initiatives, including those described above.

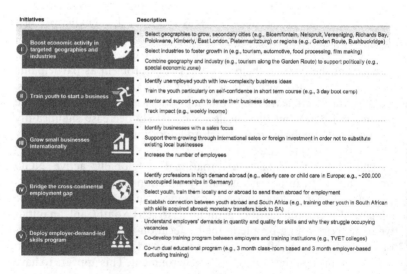

*Figure 7.3* Youth employment initiatives for South Africa.

One way to build industry and with this, jobs, is to implement a policy of import substitution – a path that South Africa started to take under the Ramaphosa administration. The other alternative is to boost exports. Logically, both should increase local employment. Regional trade and investment is yet another means to job creation. This may mean exporting local labour to countries to which companies are expanding, as in the case of South African companies opening new businesses in other African countries.

This export of labour is, however, constrained by expectations and often regulations that require these investors to hire locally in other markets in Africa. However, the African expansion has also enabled such companies to build more capacity at home to service these markets, thus creating more jobs or saving jobs when domestic demand has been low.

Thirdly, bridging the gap between jobs that are cannot be filled locally because of skills shortages and suitable candidates will also improve employment. Lastly, creating new local markets with untapped potential is another path to job creation. This could include, for example, offering products in townships that are typically only available in other areas far from these large residential areas.

Five proposals for youth employment have been developed from the research done for this book. Their validity has been tested in pilot projects. The largest hurdle to overcome in realising the different initiatives is examined, as well as the most binding constraint to implementing them.

### Proposal 1: Boosting economic activity in targeted geographies and industries

#### Concept

Boosting economic growth in targeted geographies and industries, fuelled by integration regionally and internationally, will help to address job creation. The focus should be on localised growth initiatives, as examples around the world show. Leading academic Michael Porter argues that countries do not generate a competitive advantage, but industries do, particularly where clusters of associated industries are developed.

The most famous example is probably Silicon Valley, the Information and Communication Technologies (ICT) hub developed in California. The development of cities also creates jobs and growth. Pudong, an area of Shanghai, has been transformed within just 20 years from agricultural land into a dense business district, with some of the world's highest skyscrapers. In Africa, a number of new city developments are under way to address serious congestion in colonial centres built for far fewer people than the number who have migrated there in the past few decades.

This dimension of growth is driven by two factors. One is special government incentives, such as reduced taxation or softened labour laws for companies investing in special economic zones (SEZs) or export processing zones (EPZs).

Another is a concerted focus to create a specific industrial or services hub by creating a supplier network, training focus, and logistics infrastructure. In China, Shenyang has become the automotive cluster, Nanjing is a hub for the petrochemical industry, while the Pearl River Delta (which includes Guangzhou, Shenzhen, Hong Kong, and Macao) has been developed as a manufacturing centre where consumer goods from electronics to toys and plastics are made.

Top-down prescribed approaches to building a functioning ecosystem have largely failed in Africa. A bottom-up approach involving inclusive private and public dialogues as well as partnerships is essential to creating structuralist policies that will enable economic success.

This approach can also be applied to South Africa, which already has 10 industrial development zones (IDZs) and SEZs. They include:

- Coega in Nelson Mandela Bay, which covers a range of sectors including agro-processing, automotive, aquaculture, energy, metals, logistics, and business process services.
- Richards Bay, which specialises in the manufacturing and storage of minerals and products to boost beneficiation, investment, economic growth, and develop skills and employment.
- East London for production in the automotive, agro-processing, and aquaculture sectors.
- Saldanha Bay in the Western Cape, which is an oil, gas, and marine repair engineering and logistics services complex.
- Maluti-A-Phofung (Harrismith in the Free State) for general manufacturing, focused on light and medium industry.
- OR Tambo in Ekurhuleni for the beneficiation of precious metals and minerals, with a focus on light, high-margin, export-oriented manufacturing of South African precious and semi-precious metals.
- Musina and Makhado in Limpopo near the Zimbabwean border for agro-processing and metallurgical/mineral beneficiation.

Additionally, there is the Dube Trade Port about 30 km north of Durban, which also houses the city's main airport. There are two new SEZs in in Nkomati at the border with Mozambique for agriculture, agri-processing, nutraceuticals, fertiliser production, and leather products, and the Atlantis SEZ on the west coast for the development of green technologies, alternative waste management, and alternative building materials.

As seen above, most special economic zones in South Africa do not have one particular industry focus. Also, they are not necessarily in secondary cities with potential. South Africa has failed to focus SEZs on one industry, or to locate them in and around metro areas where they would have ready access to infrastructure as well as skilled and semi-skilled labour, making them attractive to foreign investors. The success of such zones has been undermined by a top-down blanket approach, as mentioned above, rather than a bottom-up regional approach.

The South African think tank, the Centre for Development and Enterprise, developed an index for the potential of South African cities to become economic developmental zones based on population density, disposable income, and human capital levels. It listed secondary metropolitan areas with the highest potential as Emfuleni (formerly Vereeniging) with 46 points, Emalahleni (formerly Witbank) with 39 points, Msunduzi (formerly Pietermaritzburg) with 38 points, and Polokwane with 33.

Metros were ranked by decreasing potential were Johannesburg (58), City of Tshwane (53), Cape Town (49), Ekurhuleni (East Rand) 48, eThekwini (Durban) 42, Mangaung (Bloemfontein) 35, and Nelson Mandela Bay (Port Elizabeth, now renamed Gqeberha) 33.

Alexander Forbes, a financial services group, publishes a location attractiveness index ranking secondary South African cities according to returns from spill over effects based on market size, agglomeration of people and economic activity, openness of the local economy, cost of labour, quality of labour, and local stability.

The highest ranked city or municipal area on this index is uMhlathuze, which incorporates Richards Bay and Empangeni. It is followed by Emfuleni (Vereeniging and Vanderbijlpark), KwaDukuza (Ballito area), Msunduzi (Pietermaritzburg), Breede Valley (Worcester), Stellenbosch (Western Cape), Mogale City (West Rand), Drakenstein (Paarl), Metsimaholo (Sasolburg), and Saldanha Bay (Paternoster).

Again, the selection of a suitable location to build centres of economic productivity and thus jobs is crucial, but only one part of the equation. The other is what support these areas offer for an industry's needs.

South Africa does have existing industry clusters that can still be expanded. The automotive footprint in the country is large, with BMW, Chrysler, Fiat, Ford, MAN, Mercedes, Nissan, Toyota, and Volkswagen manufacturing cars mostly in northern Gauteng or in the areas around Gqeberha and East London. However, there is much more that could be done in the automotive supply chain. Why not produce seats or electronics locally, while incentivising Original Equipment Manufacturers to source local suppliers for this value chain, for example?

Tourism is already a significant industry in South Africa, contributing about 10 percent to GDP before COVID-19, as well as to employment. The upside potential for tourism is enhanced by the fact that the country has opposite seasons to the northern hemisphere, low prices by international standards, cultural diversity, many attractions, globally competitive cuisine, as well as a unique scenery, flora, and fauna. Areas such as the Kruger Park, the Garden Route, the Cape or Johannesburg, among many others, still have large untapped potential for tourism development.

The film industry is another area of potential growth. South Africa has been the location for many renowned international productions, including *Mad Max: Fury Road* (six Oscars), *Tsotsi* (Oscar, Golden Globe), and *Inxeba* (several film festival awards). The country has also been a hub for advertising. Its competitive advantage is not just its varied scenery and culture but also comparably low costs, good infrastructure, and the benefits of its weak currency for international companies.

There are many other examples of where economic development could be boosted, mostly by vertically integrating and localising value generating activities in industries such as agriculture, renewable energy, oil and gas, and metal and minerals.

The three most binding constraints to realising this potential are: trust in the South African market and political stability; the high cost of labour; and weak infrastructure outside the main business hubs.

*Pilot*

An international consulting firm is rebuilding the infrastructure along the Garden Route on South Africa's southern coastline following the massive destruction of homes and other assets in widespread fires in 2017. It has been a catalyst for several dozen direct jobs in the project itself and several hundred jobs have been saved or created in the areas of tourism and wildlife and nature preservation in the rebuilding process, strengthening the region overall and its tourism industry specifically.

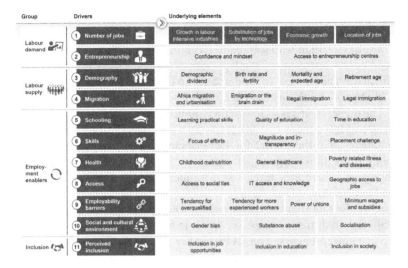

*Figure 7.4* Economic boost contribution to employment drivers.

## Proposal 2: Training youth for business

### Concept

Upskilling youth will create employment by addressing one of the key structural issues in the jobs market – a lack of suitable skills and talent.

South Africa's environment is conducive to entrepreneurship, with the existence of many entrepreneurship centres and initiatives and funding initiatives in both the private and public sectors, as highlighted in the chapter on employment drivers. However, there are gaps in this support, particularly for getting aspirant entrepreneurs onto the first rung of the ladder and to take start-ups to the next level once they have been established.

To tap into these available resources, an entrepreneur needs to have a proof of concept and an operational business. There is no structured ideation programme in South Africa to support youth at this stage. At the other end of the journey, as start-ups leave the incubation phase, there is almost no structured support to help them to scale and become small- and medium-sized enterprises (SMEs) that are able to create new jobs. These gaps undermine the ability of entrepreneurs to create much-needed jobs.

Many unemployed youths in townships do have business ideas but fail to implement them as they do not know how to run a business or how to get one off the ground. The example was used in a previous chapter of a young woman who wanted to bake and sell muffins to her community. She was not aware of available support for entrepreneurs and lacked information about how to fund and set up the business. So, she continues to sit at home thinking about her idea without a plan to make it a reality.

The question arises as to whether supporting youth entrepreneurship is a useful investment and builds the path to a viable future. Many think so. Others, like the Centre for Development and Enterprise (CDE), a policy think tank, argue that entrepreneurs are better off trained as employees, where they learn about business and get experience so they can later become self-starters.

Also, the fact that the entrepreneurial community in South Africa is relatively small means there are few role models to motivate others to become entrepreneurs. The CDE further argues that small businesses generally have a poor track record, with most failing within five years of registration.

But notwithstanding these arguments, sometimes all that is needed is sufficient support for someone to start a small venture that may not transform into a company or create new jobs but may at least offer that person a path to earn some money. It is this model that drives many self-employed people in South Africa.

Lastly, longevity is typically related to registered businesses. Most of the start-up businesses in townships are informal and do not appear in formal statistics, nor do they pay tax. However, as these businesses grow, there is greater incentive for them to become formalised, particularly to access B-BBEE opportunities.

Businesses started by unemployed youth may not scale, but they show young people that economic activity pays as it enables them to earn money. This is the first step on the ladder.

It is arguable whether young people starting their own business create net new jobs. On the one hand, they stimulate a chain of economic activity, for example by purchasing goods outside the township for sale in the streets of their home area. This activity helps to create a new market and add incremental value, which may spawn a few jobs down the line. But they need to start on the business journey to create any value. The case of the young woman who wanted to start a muffin business triggered the author to initiate a programme to support her and others like her, as illustrated in the pilot outline below.

Research in Africa has shown that entrepreneurs trained in soft skills help to successfully incubate the business more than those who have

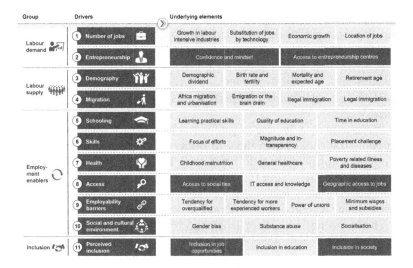

*Figure 7.5* Entrepreneurship boot camp's contribution to employment drivers.

undertaken hard-skills business training. Field work has also shown that self-confidence is the largest challenge for youth, who have typically failed multiple times throughout their lives, dropping out of school and not being successful with job applications.

## Pilot

In collaboration with Khonology, an employment and IT consultancy, the author developed a three-day entrepreneurship boot camp to train youths that were keen to start a business. The applicants had to be unemployed South Africans with a simple business idea and a sound motivation. The selected entrepreneurs-to-be were invited to train for three days.

B-BBEE does support registered small enterprises through preferential procurement and hiring practices and the programme provides support for enterprise development. However, youth targeted by the above-mentioned boot camp would likely set up non-registered businesses and would not qualify for that support.

The main requirement for the boot camp to be a success was to have a reliable, competent, and nationally represented partner for the rollout, with access to a recruitment pipeline for the youth, training and train-the-trainer capabilities, and rigorous monitoring and evaluation capacity.

The training covered three main exercises. The first was to increase the motivation of the participants and to determine whether they had the right personality profile to start a business. The second was to check whether a participant had the right skills for his/her business idea, interacting with potential customers, and getting feedback on the business idea. The third, was inviting successful entrepreneurs as guest speakers to be role models for participants and to define next steps and milestones.

Participants would have to get feedback on their business plan from random strangers to help them to overcome the fear of approaching people unknown to them to pitch their idea, and getting immediate unfiltered feedback. After the three days, each participant was allocated a mentor as well as references for further support, including links to useful online resources and entrepreneurship centres.

The 11 business ideas the participants brought to the boot camp were starting up a driving school, making and selling children's clothing, setting up a fitness studio, establishing an internet café, starting an interior design business, doing family coaching, delivering fruit, setting up an e-commerce platform, stationery delivery, starting an IT training centre, and establishing a customer service consultancy.

Five entrepreneurs started earning money a month after they finished the training. The young man who wanted to start a fitness studio was hesitant, due to a lack of funds to rent a venue and buy equipment. The entrepreneurship boot camp helped him to iterate his idea. Within the training course, he met the commissioner of the local police station, who offered to pay him to train policemen. In the end, no investment was required for him to get started.

This concept, originated by the author, can be easily rolled out to make it accessible for many more youth as the pilot has proved.

### Proposal 3: Growing SMEs

*Concept*
Growing SMEs allows for job creation by integrating South African businesses into local and international value chains, thereby boosting the local economy.

However, the South African entrepreneurial environment lacks support for small but growing companies despite the fact that the South African National Development Plan for 2030 identifies SMEs as the engine of job growth in the country. The plan forecasts that SMEs will create 90 percent of new jobs by 2030, with 11 million jobs being created by 49,000 SMEs. This suggests growth of 20 percent a year.

This is undoubtedly an ambitious assumption, especially considering South Africa's stagnant economy and low growth, which spilled over into economic recession in early 2020. It is also overly ambitious given the lack of a supportive ecosystem as noted above. For example, it is difficult for smaller food suppliers to get their goods onto the shelves of the major retailers as their supply chains are difficult to break into.

The McKinsey Global Institute, a think tank, identified the sectors with the largest job creation potential as being advanced manufacturing (such as the automotive and defence industries), agriculture (production and processing), and service exports (such as international call centres). In these target industries alone, about 2,500 new jobs are possible until 2030 based on their projected contribution to GDP.

The country's new local content programme is an opportunity for small- to medium-sized businesses to enter local supply and value chains, for example by producing inputs for the manufacturing industry. Exporting food is an opportunity under the African Continental Free Trade Area (AfCFTA). These opportunities could lead to job growth but for this to be a reality, such companies would need more support for their go-to-market strategy, cash-flow optimisation, and operational improvements and other barriers to success and scale.

B-BBEE could be a useful leg up for SMEs wanting to participate in local content, or import substitution, initiatives but perhaps less so for those wanting to increase exports as their engagement is with customers outside national borders who have no interest in their suppliers' empowerment credentials and benefits. But benefiting from the country's empowerment legislation is not a sufficient criterion for success as companies still need to have the vision, skills, and markets to take advantage of the enterprise development opportunities offered by large companies to incorporate B-BBEE beneficiaries into their supply chains. These same companies may also be competition for newer and smaller entrants.

The most binding constraint to accelerate the growth of SMEs is the recruiting of companies to train and build the capabilities of SMEs to provide industry-specific expertise.

## Pilot

The South African branch of a global consulting firm has implemented such a model as an element of pro-bono programme. Participating SMEs received pro-bono consulting advice for a short period of time, and the managers of several SMEs were trained in the fields of go-to-market strategy, cash-flow optimisation, and operational optimisation.

*Figure 7.6* SME accelerator contribution to employment drivers.

This allowed them to create incremental revenue to support the hiring of about 500 new employees across the companies within less than nine months after starting the programme. This success illustrates that there is significant potential for creating new jobs incrementally.

### Proposal 4: Bridging the cross-continental employment gap

*Concept*

Cross-continental bridging creates employment by matching labour market needs, moving labour to where it is most needed.

There are global disparities when it comes to labour supply and demand. Aging societies lack the youth to fill jobs while other countries with high youth populations experience severe unemployment. Germany, for example, has a challenge because of its aging population. Already in 2016, close to 200,000 learnerships were unoccupied in Germany. One area where labour shortages are significant is caregiving.

People are living longer, which is increasing demand for care, but there is little appetite among young people in Germany for this type of employment. By 2030, 300,000 caregivers will be needed, 200,000 of them in elderly care.

At the same time, there are many unemployed or underemployed but qualified caregivers in South Africa, such as qualified community health workers. Bridging this gap would allow South African youth to gain training, employment, and international exposure while addressing the caregiving gap in Germany. Additionally, the German and South African governments could both address their social responsibility burdens through such an exchange.

The biggest challenge to implementing this initiative would be the support of the government in the receiving country. Issues it would need to consider include immigration regulations, the capacity and inter-cultural competency of the training providers in the receiving country, and how best to source resilient youths who would want to learn another language and tackle the challenges of relocation abroad.

## *Pilot*

The uNowanga project, launched in South Africa in 2019 to address South Africa's high youth unemployment rate, has made this issue its purpose. uNowanga is the isiZulu and isiXhosa name for the white stork that travels from Europe to Africa and back, as would the caregivers in the model described above. It was initiated by the author of this book

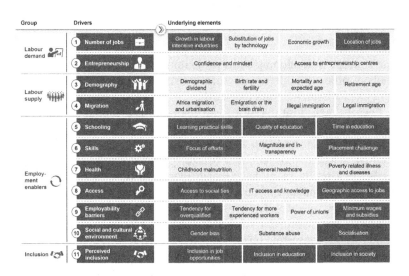

*Figure 7.7* Cross-continental bridging contribution to employment drivers.

and the CEO of the Order of St John, an order of chivalry focusing on healthcare in South Africa and many other countries. The programme is a joint venture between the Order of St John and the Johanniter Order, its German equivalent.

The Order of St John trains youth from mostly disadvantaged backgrounds to become community health workers. This accredited programme allows these young people to earn a small stipend in their local community. As the stipend is low – between R1,800 and R2,200 per month – they are technically regarded as being unemployed.

uNowanga recruits from this pool of people for a four-year programme. For the first 12 months, the recruits learn German and work in a German old-age home in South Africa co-run by the Johanniter Order. After qualifying in German, they do an apprenticeship in Germany at a Johanniter old age home, qualifying as a nurse (Kranken-und Altenplfeger in German). After three years, their apprenticeship is concluded, qualifying them to work as a nurse in Germany or in South Africa.

The successful candidates benefit from a new qualification from a fully funded programme, international experience, and upward mobility. They may return to South Africa with skills in high demand back home, creating a brain gain in the healthcare industry, which more typically is affected by a brain drain as qualified professionals emigrate to seek jobs elsewhere.

### Proposal 5: Employer demand-led skills programmes

*Concept*

The concept is developing skills programmes that are led by employer needs in order to address structural unemployment caused by insufficient employability among the youth.

Even though South Africa faces high youth unemployment, companies still struggle to find talent, particularly qualified workers. Companies cannot rely on the school system, nor on tertiary education, to produce sufficient numbers of suitable candidates for their needs. As a result, many have set up their own training facilities. For example, Steinmüller in South Africa, the supplier of components for power plants, operates its own training centre. This is a cost-intensive but necessary investment to enable them to execute to the required standards. This investment is risky, given the tendency for companies to poach competitors' talent in an environment of skills shortages.

The need for companies to bring skills training in house may have many benefits for the company, and for skills development in the country, but it also adds to South Africa's already high labour costs. This affects the country's overall competitiveness, particularly compared to other African countries, which tend to have less unionisation and lower labour costs.

Technical, vocational, and digital skills are the hardest to find and often the costliest to develop because of the investment in training and the high salaries they can demand in an environment of scarcity. Quality manual skills ought to be provided by public and private TVET colleges, but these institutions are not up to standard, often using outdated curricula and machinery to train students. This means many graduates are unable to meet the needs of modern employers.

Digital skills, such as specialised developers, are typically provided by universities. However, their training is more generic. Institutions that purely focus on programming skills are few, but the ones that exist have absorption rates of close to 100 percent. The above highlights two problems. The first is a lack of training capacity to meet the demand for digital skills, while the second is a lack of quality training in vocational colleges.

How does the system operate currently? The structural foundation for vocational training is solid. South Africa offers three pathways to vocational training, namely the National Certificate (Vocational), the Nated System, and the Occupational Sub-framework. The funding for these is secured, although there are bureaucratic hurdles to manage. TVET colleges are funded and accredited by the government's vocational skills training organisation, the Sector Education and Training Authority. There are 21 of these and they cover every main industry and occupation in the country, funded in part by the skills development levy paid by employers, which is an element of their B-BBEE spend. TVETs tend to train mostly in the professions that attract the largest funding and not necessarily those with the largest need. They have also failed to invest sufficiently in the modernisation and upgrading of training and curricula.

The multitude of training providers – about 8,000 offer a magnitude of professions and job options – often leave youth facing tough choices about which path to take. They may lack insight into which capabilities they may need for a job and what sort of skills to pursue. When it comes to training, youths often face costs such as the costs and availability of transportation or tuition.

The system does not deliver its mandate efficiently because of a disconnect between employers, skills training, and the youth. School leavers are not given an appreciation of the value of vocational training. Career guidance is poor, and many do not know where to get further

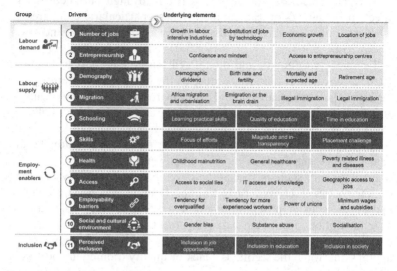

*Figure 7.8* Employer demand-led training contribution to employment drivers.

education, and which jobs offer the best career path. Employers and educational institutions do not engage on what the marketplace needs and companies tend to lack empathy for the challenges of the youth, such as transport costs and reliability.

The disconnect carries through from training to recruitment. In the recruiting process, youths often lack an overview of training opportunities and promising jobs with a good chance of employment and decent pay. They tend to see manual labour, and thus vocational training, as a last resort. Training providers face the challenge of changing this perception and attracting youth to the vocational training on offer. Employers do little to change this perception, even those that require such skills.

Further to this, the workplace exposure is not necessarily built into the curricula. Employers see the workplace component of the training as an additional cost burden along with the skills levy and additional management and supervision effort, without seeing the bigger picture. They do not always understand the challenges the youth has in getting to the stage of applying for a job.

Young people tend to lack support structures for finding a job after they finish training. The training provider cannot always help, often lacking the networks in the job market.

A multifaceted approach is needed to solve these problems. All stakeholders – the youth, employers, schools, and training institutions – need to engage to develop a scalable and feasible financing model, tapping into government funding streams as well as corporate support. Work also needs to be done to shift the mindset of young people who can afford post-school training to see the value of apprenticeships, rather than only aspiring to attend university.

*Pilot*

The solution to this challenge is not to simply roll out more training options or better skills development, nor just to get more young people to attend TVETs. As long as the placement rates are low, this would merely create a shift would be from unqualified unemployed young people to qualified unemployed youth, with significant costs involved in the process.

The solution is a demand-led skills programme, integrating youth, training providers, and employers. First, employers need to have a forward-looking talent strategy, rather than relying on ad hoc and often spontaneous recruitment. They could then link up with training providers to state their needs and make input into a more relevant vocational training curriculum, incorporating classroom and on-the-job training.

The on-the-job training would allow the youth and the employer to assess whether a working relationship after the training is in their common interest. Using government and available third-party funding, the employer would be able to cover additional costs to train as many young people as required, in addition to the existing employer subsidy they have to pay. Thirdly, employers and training providers could jointly highlight the programme's benefits, including a high likelihood of placement after the successful completion of the curriculum.

This type of programme is similar to a German or Swiss apprenticeship model. McKinsey and Company's GENERATION programme, a private vocational training programme set up in various countries around the world, delivers a very similar approach. It targets countries in which the public system does not have a strong structural foundation for vocational training. It has been rolled out in Australia, Hong Kong, India, Italy, Kenya, Mexico, Pakistan, Singapore, Spain, the United Kingdom, and the United States, covering 93 cities on 234 sites, and absorbing 82 percent of trainees within 90 days of their completing the programme.

## Bibliography

Asche, H., & Grimm, M. (2017). Industrialisation in Africa: Challenges and opportunities. *PEGNet Policy Briefs, 8/2017.*

Bernstein, A. (2004). *Key to growth: Supporting South Africa's emerging entrepreneurs* (12th ed.). *Policy in the Making.* Johannesburg: CDE.

City Press (2019, January 19). SA's 10 industrial and special economic zones. *City Press*, p. 7.

DTI (2018). *Special economic zone (SEZ).* Department: Trade, Industry and Competition

Handelsblatt (2016). *Knapp 200.000 Ausbildungsplätze unbesetzt.* [online].

Hausmann, R., Klinger, B., & Wagner, R. (2008). Doing growth diagnostics in practice: A 'Mindbook'. *Center for International Development at Harvard University, 177.*

Hausmann, R., Rodrik, D., & Velasco, A. (2008). Growth diagnostics. In Narcís Serra and Joseph E. Stiglitz (Eds.) *The Washington consensus reconsidered: Towards a new global governance*, 324–355. Oxford Scholarship [online].

McKinsey & Company (2017). *Dance of the lions and dragons: How are Africa and China engaging, and how will the partnership evolve?* McKinsey & Company.

McKinsey Global Institute (June 2010). *Lions on the move: The progress and potential of African economies.* Retrieved from www.mckinsey.com/global-themes/middle-east-and-africa/lions-on-the-move

McKinsey Global Institute (2012). *Africa at work: Job creation and inclusive growth.* McKinsey & Company.

McKinsey Global Institute (September 2016). *Lions on the move II: Realizing the potential of Africa's economies.* McKinsey & Company.

McKinsey Global Institute (2018). Notes from the frontier: Modelling the impact of AI on the world economy. *Discussion Paper.*

NDP (2011). *National development plan.* Pretoria: National Planning Commission.

Oxford Economics (2018). *Country economic forecasts: South Africa.* [online].

Porter, M. (1990). The competitive advantage of nations. *Harvard Business Review, 68*(2), 73–93.

Schirmer, S., & Bernstein, A. (2017). *Business, growth and inclusion: Tackling youth unemployment in cities, towns and townships.* Johannesburg: CDE.

Stalinski, S. (2017). *Überlastet, ausgebrannt - und weg: Pflegenotstand in Deutschland.* Tagesschau (online presence of TV programme).

Expert interviews

Participating observations

Websites of mentioned organisations

# 8   Winter is (not) coming

Is *Winter* coming to South Africa? Will the worst-case scenario happen? May the country be fortunate and have *Summer* in 2040, or will it face *Spring* or *Fall*? This all depends on how the youth employment challenge is handled in the present.

In the introduction, this work discusses the idea of a "ticking time bomb." It asks a number of questions. Why is there a bomb with a ticking detonator in the first place? What happens when it explodes? When will the timer run out and trigger the detonation? Can it be defused? How? By whom?

The first question is easily answered. There is a bomb that could explode because more than half of South Africa's youth is unemployed today. The numbers may change, but the situation is not new; it has been building up over decades and is deeply rooted in the economic and societal structure of both apartheid and post-apartheid South Africa.

As a result, there is no quick or easy way to solve this problem, and the youth are aware of that. They know they have limited access to education, limited access to job opportunities, and therefore limited opportunity to become part of the economic fabric of the country.

But there is hope. The middle class is growing as the poor move up the social ladder. But this trend needs to gain critical mass to make a difference. Unfulfilled hopes and dreams, and a violent response to the frustration this causes, are what may trigger the bomb. Not finding the first rung of the ladder to a better life, or not being able to climb that ladder, is leading young people down the path of despair and frustration. That is the dynamite in the bomb.

What happens when it explodes? When the timer stops and triggers a detonation, the youth will rise up and fight for what they think is their right: becoming part of the society by gaining access to opportunities and even land or property in proximity to economic hubs.

DOI: 10.4324/9781003186052-9

Ultimately, what will happen between now and 2040 is uncertain. The four scenarios, however, give an indication of what is possible, and even likely, depending on different drivers. And only one scenario – *Spring* – involves an explosive situation, or the metaphorical detonation.

*Spring* may not be a worst-case scenario as a youth revolt has the potential to trigger change in society for the better, as seen in the Arab Spring. But, as events in North Africa since the uprising have shown, it is still a long journey to a more stable and prosperous society after the dust has settled on a major political uprising.

South Africa has had a taste of what such an insurrection could look like. In July 2021, hundreds of people went on the rampage in the province of KwaZulu-Natal and parts of Gauteng, an uprising driven by politically motivated messaging related to the incarceration of former president Zuma at the time. Hundreds of people invaded stores, offices, warehouses, and shopping malls in a frenzy of looting and violence in which more than 300 people died and infrastructure was damaged or destroyed. This was an unsettling "Spring storm" and possibly a portent of the future.

Can the bomb be defused? How? By whom? Yes, it can! There is hope for South Africa, but the path to *Summer* is long, windy, stony, and steep, and requires immense resilience and perseverance to walk. Access to the ladder to opportunity and inclusion needs to be widened – and fast.

The five proposed initiatives – targeted economic growth, entrepreneurship support, SME growth, international opportunities, and an employer-demand-led training programme – are the foundations of this increased access. Once the foundation has been laid, new jobs will be created, which will improve peoples' lives. To achieve this, all South Africans need to join forces, including government, the private sector, the schools and training providers, the rich, the poor, the middle class, the employed, and the unemployed.

# Index

Printed in the United States
by Baker & Taylor Publisher Services